Jean-François Lyotard

Modern **C**ultural **T**heorists

Jean-François Lyotard

Stuart Sim

PRENTICE HALL
HARVESTER WHEATSHEAF

LONDON   NEW YORK   TORONTO   SYDNEY   TOKYO   SINGAPORE
MADRID   MEXICO CITY   MUNICH

First published 1996 by
Prentice Hall/Harvester Wheatsheaf
Campus 400, Maylands Avenue
Hemel Hempstead
Hertfordshire, HP2 7EZ
A division of
Simon & Schuster International Group

Typeset in 11/12pt Ehrhardt
by Dorwyn Ltd, Rowlands Castle, Hampshire

Printed and bound in Great Britain by
Biddles Ltd, Guildford and King's Lynn

Library of Congress Cataloging in Publication Data

Sim, Stuart.
　Jean-François Lyotard/Stuart Sim.
　　p.　cm. — (Modern cultural theorists)
　　Includes bibliographical references and index.
　　ISBN 0-13-433434-5
　　　1. Lyotard, Jean François.　I. Title.　II. Series.
　B2430.L964S55　1995
　194—dc20　　　　　　　　　　　　　　　　95-34295
　　　　　　　　　　　　　　　　　　　　　　CIP

British Library Cataloguing in Publication Data

A catalogue record for this book is available from
the British Library

ISBN 0–13–433434–5

1　2　3　4　5　　　00　99　98　97　96

To my sister Fiona,
in memory of our mother

Contents

Acknowledgements

I would like to express my thanks to the School of Arts, Design and Communications at the University of Sunderland for providing me with sabbatical time to help complete this project. Thanks too to Dr Helene Brandon for bearing up through yet another publishing project.

Abbreviated titles list

DF	*Discours, figure*
Diff	*The Differend*
DT	*Duchamp's Trans/Formers*
Hj	*Heidegger and 'the jews'*
JG	*Just Gaming*
In	*The Inhuman*
LAS	*Lessons on the Analytic of the Sublime*
LE	*Libidinal Economy*
LR	*Lyotard Reader*
Per	*Peregrinations: Law, Form, Event*
PC	*The Postmodern Condition*
PW	*Political Writings*
Ph	*Phenomenology*
TP	*Toward the Postmodern*

Chronology

1924	Born Versailles
1948	First substantial publication, 'Nés en 1925', appears in *Les Temps Modernes*
1950–52	Teacher of philosophy at high school in Constantine, Algeria
1952–59	Teaching at Prytanée militaire de la Flèche
1954	Joins *Socialisme ou barbarie* group; *Phenomenology*
1955	Takes over responsibility for Algerian 'section' in the journal *Socialisme ou barbarie*
1955–62	Regular commentator on Algerian question in *Socialisme ou barbarie* (articles to appear later in *La Guerre des Algeriens*)
1959–66	Teaching at University of Paris
1964	Schism in *Socialisme ou barbarie*; Lyotard joins breakaway *Pouvoir Ouvrier* group
1966	Resigns from *Pouvoir Ouvrier*
1966–70	Teaching at University of Nanterre
1968	Organizes demonstrations at University of Nanterre during revolutionary *événements*
1970–72	Teaching at University of Paris VIII, Vincennes
1971	*Discours, figure*
1972–87	Professor of Philosophy at the University of Paris VIII, Vincennes
1973	*Des dispositifs pulsionnels*; *Dérive à partir de Marx et Freud*
1974	*Libidinal Economy*
1974–76	Visiting Professor, University of California at San Diego and Berkeley, and at Johns Hopkins University, Baltimore

1976   Senior Fellow, University of Wisconsin
1977   *Instructions païennes*; *Rudiments païens: genre dissertatif*; *Duchamp's Trans/Formers*; *Récits tremblants*
1978–80   Visiting Professor, University of São-Paulo, Brazil, and University of Montreal
1979   *Just Gaming*; *The Postmodern Condition*; *Le Mur du pacifique*
1980   *Sur la constitution du temps par la couleur dans les oeuvres récentes d'Albert Ayme*
1983   Helps found the Collège Internationale de Philosophie in Paris; *The Differend*
1984   *L'Assassinat de l'experience par la peinture: Monory*; *Tombeau de l'intellectuel et autres papiers*; *Driftworks*
1984–86   President, International College of Philosophy, Paris
1985   Organizes art exhibition, *Les Immatériaux*, at the Pompidou Centre, Paris
1986   Gives Wellek Library Lectures at the University of California, Irvine (later published as *Peregrinations: Law, Form, Event*); continues involvement with University of California at Irvine as Distinguished Professor in the French Department and Critical Theory Program; *The Postmodern Explained to Children: Correspondence 1982–1985*; *L'Enthousiasme: la critique kantienne de l'histoire*; Visiting Professor, University of Minnesota
1987   *Que Peindre? Adami Arakawa Buren*
1988   *Peregrinations: Law, Event, Form*; *The Inhuman: Reflections on Time*; *Heidegger and 'the jews'*; *La Guerre des Algeriens: Écrits 1956–63*; Visiting Professor, University of Seigen, Germany
1989   *The Lyotard Reader*; Visiting Professor, University of New York, Binghamton
1990   Senior Fellow, University of Aarhus, Denmark; Visiting Professor, University of New York, Stony Brook
1991   *Lessons on the Analytic of the Sublime*; *Lectures d'enfance*; Senior Fellow, University of Turin
1992   Visiting Professor, Yale University
1993   *Moralités postmodernes*
1993–95   Visiting Professor, Emory University, Atlanta

Preface

Any commentator who sets out to track the career of a postmodernist theorist such as Jean-François Lyotard immediately finds him or herself in an awkward position, in trying to present as a coherent body of work what its creator wishes to remain disparate and amorphous (not to mention his defenders, for whom there are many and various 'Lyotards' in a publishing career 'more remarkable for its shifts and breaks than for any continuity', as Geoffrey Bennington has put it[1]). Here is a writer who argues that the 'grand narratives' (or universal theories) of the West have collapsed, including, incidentally, the grand narrative of rational explanation derived from the 'Enlightenment project', so called – exactly what a volume of this kind finds itself engaged in.

Surely the mere fact of presenting Lyotard's life and thought as if it had some kind of internal logic to it – in fact, precisely to *seek* such an internal logic – is to have missed the whole point of postmodernism? This is, after all, the man who proclaims apocalyptically of his fellow theorists of the postmodern that, 'We deliver no message, we bear no truth, bring no revelation, and we do not speak for those who remain silent',[2] the man who resists the idea of a pattern to events, who denies any virtue to the art of critique and commentary ('there is *no analysis*: not even Freud's' (*LE*, p. 259)). To attempt to render Lyotard, therefore, is to attempt what postmodernism tells us cannot be done. It is, to the postmodernist mind anyway, to signal oneself as remaining in thrall to the comforting illusions of the modern – that outmoded and unjustifiably optimistic world-view which the postmodern has long since eclipsed.

One possible strategy for the inveterate believer in critique and commentary is to treat Lyotard as an exemplary figure, a theorist whose career, with its various twists and turns of intellectual direction from the 1940s to the 1990s, can be read as an enactment of Western thought in a period of accelerated cultural crisis. Thus the shifting positions of Lyotard's thought demonstrate the *necessity* for the development of postmodernism as the current theoretical paradigms, for a variety of reasons, systematically fail him at critical junctures – the Algerian Revolution, and the 1968 Paris revolutionary *événements* being cases in point. Faced with large-scale disjunctions of theory and practice – a Marxism which cannot really comprehend the unique nature of the Algerian Revolution, a Communist Party which cannot countenance a truly subversive revolutionary fervour in the Paris of 1968 – Lyotard is forced to think the unthinkable: that his cultural paradigm has irretrievably broken down and that none of his beliefs will stand up to much close scrutiny. In Lyotard's case the postmodern begins with an act of loss of faith in an entire cultural tradition and its considerable array of assumptions: a loss of faith extreme enough for one of his defenders to claim that, after 1968, Lyotard 'is not a theorist' in that he comes to regard theory 'as part of the problem, not as a potential solution'[3] (not a particularly helpful position to adopt in my opinion, and a further indication of the obstacles that Lyotard discipleship can set in our way).

It is the context, and then the implications, of that loss of faith that will concern us in this volume. Postmodernism can all too often appear a superficial and facile discourse, a matter of modish gesture and the striking of attitudes rather than deep thought and emotional turmoil (rather unfortunately for him, Jean Baudrillard almost always comes to mind at such moments), but in Lyotard's case we can see the development of the postmodern temperament as it is 'felt on the pulses', and it is in that honesty of response that much of his attraction as a theorist lies.

The reader will see a certain kind of narrative developing already, in which it is likely that some texts of Lyotard will loom larger than others for purposes of analysis (although every effort will be made to give an overall sense of his work and its key concepts and concerns). It is not the only narrative that can be derived from Lyotard's career of course, but I believe that it is a reasonably fruitful one if we are to try to come to terms with this complex, wide-ranging and highly productive thinker. Chapters 1–5 will trace the development of Lyotard's postmodernism against the backgound of his tortuous relationship to Marxist theory; Chapters 6–9 will concentrate on certain key aspects and recurrent themes of his writing (svelteness, paganism, the sublime, art and aesthetics, intellectuals, for example); Chapter 10 and the conclusion will explore Lyotard's later writing in the perspective of his long and distinguished career and its many 'shifts and breaks'.

Historical and cultural context

Jean-François Lyotard was born in Versailles in 1924 and has had a distinguished academic career in both France and America, holding professorships at the University of Paris, Vincennes, and the University of California at Irvine, as well as a string of visiting professorships around the world. He was also one of the founding members of the prestigious, and controversial, Collège Internationale de Philosophie in Paris (Jacques Derrida being one of the others), a research institution set up with French government money to explore the more esoteric areas of modern philosophical enquiry. His publishing career now spans almost fifty years and he is widely, and justifiably, regarded as one of the most creative thinkers of the later twentieth century, a philosopher and cultural theorist of impressive scope whose considerable body of writings has helped to change the intellectual landscape of his time. That intellectual landscape, and Lyotard's place within it, will now be considered briefly.

Lyotard's name is now indissolubly connected with the cultural movement known as postmodernism, and his seminal study *The Postmodern Condition: A Report on Knowledge* (1979) has turned out to be one of the most heavily cited books of the late twentieth century, but he is far more than just a proselytizer for the brave new world of postmodernity. This survey takes as its brief to communicate something of the breadth and richness of Lyotard's oeuvre, and to present him, as indicated in the Preface, as an exemplar of cultural change: someone whose thinking *enacts* the problem of the postmodern as much as it theorizes or celebrates it, and whose range of concerns and interventions in various long-running debates (such as that about foundations of discourse) should ensure him a lasting place in philosophical history.

The intellectual landscape of the last half-century, particularly in France, has undergone some dramatic changes, in many of which Lyotard has been a leading actor. He is part of a generation which was heavily infected by the doctrines of Marxism, and in fact until very recently it was hardly possible *not* to be in dialogue with Marxism if one were a French intellectual or academic. Marxism in effect formed the horizon of intellectual debate in France in the aftermath of the Second World War, and no intellectual or academic of the time could avoid having to confront the theory at some point in their careers. Some kind of a dialogue with Marxism, which is not the same thing as acquiescence with the theory of course, was almost a condition of existence for the post-war French intellectual. One has only to think of Jean-Paul Sartre, far and away the most important French thinker in the immediate postwar years, vainly trying to reconcile the not very complementary doctrines of existentialism and Marxism to realize how deep an impression the latter theory had made on the French intellectual scene. Lyotard himself in his first book, *Phenomenology* (1954), tried to establish some grounds for cooperation between phenomenology and Marxism, despite his own recognition of 'the *insurmountable* oppositions' that separated the two theories.[1] Even Jacques Derrida, whose work has seemed to strive to keep politics at arm's length over a period of decades, has, as late as the 1990s, felt it necessary to engage with Marx and his legacy (if in Derrida's characteristically eccentric way).[2]

A broad overview of the last half-century would reveal a general sympathy towards Marxism amongst French intellectuals for the first two decades or so, despite some misgivings as to the French Communist Party's (PCF) policy over the 'Algerian question' (the long-running war of liberation in what was then France's major colony), followed by progressive disenchantment from 1968 onwards when the PCF was widely felt to have sold out to its political enemies in order to bring about an end to the *événements* of that year. In the wake of these events come a host of theories – poststructuralism, postmodernism, various versions of feminism – which challenge Marxism's intellectual supremacy, either directly or indirectly, and which mark a turn away from politics in its traditional, party-oriented form. Lyotard, as we shall see, was one of those whose disenchantment with dialectical materialism turned into direct challenge.

If Marxism formed the horizon for most French intellectuals in the period under discussion, many other theories also vied for their attention within that horizon. Existentialism, phenomenology and structuralism are the most obvious to note, and the first two certainly have left their impression on Lyotard's thought, often in surprising and unexpected ways. The doyen of existentialism was Sartre, and his individual subject-centred theory had a profound influence on postwar Western thought. Existentialism became something of a cult in France, particularly in Paris, and a whole generation of French philosophers came under Sartre's considerable influence; it is noteworthy in this respect that Lyotard's first substantial publication, 'Nés en 1925' (1947) was published in Sartre's journal *Les Temps Modernes*.

The world as pictured by Sartrean existentialism is one of absurdity, a world into which we are 'abandoned' as individuals into a contingent and isolated existence. The Sartrean individual is a free agent, in the sense that he or she always has the freedom, even if it is often of a severely limited kind ('do this' or 'don't do this', for example), to make choices no matter what situation he or she may find themselves in. All around the individual, however, lurks the constant threat of nothingness, or non-being, which is constantly poised to engulf the individual 'being-for-itself'. Sartre was not the first French thinker to present such a picture of the 'free' individual, and it can also be seen in the work of several pre- and postwar dramatists and novelists, such as Anouilh and Gide, but none presented it in quite so melodramatic a form as Sartre, and it was a form which proved to have a widespread appeal for a disoriented postwar society. Something of that melodramatic individualism echoes through the work of thinkers as diverse, and ostensibly post- or even anti-existentialist, as Foucault, Derrida, and Lyotard. There is at the very least the echo of that existentialist freedom in Lyotard's 'svelte' individual, 'svelteness' being that condition of personal flexibility where, in Lyotard's memorable phrase, 'one goes to a ball in the evening, and one wages war the next day at dawn in the morning'.[3] 'Svelteness' also contains echoes of the Sartrean concept of the *engagé* individual, who endeavours to find a way out of the impasse of personal isolation by collective political action and commitment to a common cause.

Existentialism is rooted in phenomenology, and many of the ideas to be found in Sartre's major philosophical work *Being and Nothingness* are in fact derived from Heidegger's earlier phenomenological researches (see *Being and Time*, for example). Phenomenology constitutes another of the critical theoretical influences on French intellectual life since the postwar period (many commentators have seen it as the defining characteristic of what has come to be known as 'continental philosophy'), and it continues to exert a major impact through the work of such phenomenologically based thinkers as Derrida and Lyotard. Phenomenology's search for an unproblematical starting-point (or 'foundation') for philosophical discourse, as well as for a method of analysis free from presuppositions (such as God, absolute truth or any other form of transcendental signified) resonates throughout French thought from Sartre onwards and Lyotard is no exception, his first book, *Phenomenology*, being a survey of the ideas of such major figures in the history of the phenomenological movement as Husserl and Merleau-Ponty. It is worth mentioning that one of Lyotard's major objections to phenomenology is its tendency towards ahistoricality, suggesting that even at this early stage in his career he is very alive to the political and ethical dimensions of philosophical theory (some commentators have claimed to find links between the analytical style of this work and Lyotard's later postmodernist offerings[4]).

The incorporation of phenomenology is taken to be one of the hallmarks of modern French philosophy and Lyotard is very much of his time in retaining a phenomenological dimension to his thought throughout his career (for all that he can be very critical of the theory on occasion, especially in later life), but it remains Marxism which is responsible for the most dramatic shifts in his theoretical perspective. Lyotard was a member for several years of the *Socialisme ou barbarie* group, a collective of Marxist thinkers dedicated, in the pages of the journal of the same name, to conducting a critique of Marxism from inside the theory itself: 'carrying on the Marxist critique of reality, both theoretical and practical', as

Lyotard put it, 'even to its extreme consequences' ('The Name of Algeria', *PW*, p. 171). Within the group, which included such other important thinkers on the left as Cornelius Castoriadis and Claude Lefort, Lyotard's role was, from 1955 onwards, to be the specialist commentator on Algeria, where he had in fact spent some time working as a schoolteacher in the early 1950s.

Lyotard's writings on Algeria, which will be considered in more detail in Chapter 1, take place against a background of bloody colonial war which dragged on from the 1950s (1955 saw the declaration by the French Chamber of Deputies of a state of emergency in Algeria) through to the foundation of an independent Algerian state in 1962. The Algerian war revealed deep divisions within French society, and Lyotard is very much an active participator in the debates generated by France's swift decline as a colonial power (the loss of Indochina also occurring during the same period), thus giving the lie, as Bill Readings notes in his Introduction to Lyotard's collected political writings, to the notion that 'poststructuralism is an evasion of politics, or that Lyotard's account of the postmodern condition is the product of blissful ignorance of the postcolonial question' (*PW*, p. xiii). At least some part of Lyotard's disenchantment with grand narratives and the nation state can be traced back to his experience as a political commentator during this troubled phase of modern French history, where he is already complaining about the many compromises made by the Communists with the ruling authorities at the expense of the working classes.

1968 provided yet another source of disenchantment for Lyotard. He was active as a political militant during the May *événements* organizing protests at the University of Nanterre, and was immediately critical of the pattern of events which saw the insurrection peter out, at least in part because of the lukewarm support offered the revolutionary-minded strikers, militant students and intellectuals by the PCF. The ending of the *événements* in nothing more dramatic than a general increase in wage levels (whereas for Lyotard it had represented a desire for a fundamental change in social relations), called Marxism's credibility seriously into question, and the theory thereafter went into slow, but steady decline amongst the French intellectual community.

Even so, Marxism remained a powerful force in French intellectual life, and a source of constant and intense debate. Throughout the 1960s and 1970s Althusser's reformulation of Marxism along the lines of structuralist theory, 'structural Marxism' as it was known, had a considerable vogue. Althusser was one of the towering presences in Western thought of this period, and his revision of Marxist theory in works such as *Reading Capital* and *For Marx* was the source of a mini-industry of comment and critique on the left in the English-speaking world no less than in France.[5] Structural Marxism, like all forms of structuralism, increasingly came under attack as the 1970s progressed, and Lyotard could be quite contemptuous about all such revisions of Marxist theory; as he remarks witheringly in *Libidinal Economy*:

> We no longer want to correct Marx, to reread him or to read him in the sense that the little Althusserians would like to 'read *Capital*': to interpret it according to 'its truth'. We have no plan to be true, to give the truth of Marx, we wonder what there is of libido in Marx. (p. 97)

Lyotard's bitter reaction to Althusser reveals him to be very much in the vanguard of poststructuralism.

One of the ways that the poststructuralist reaction to structuralism, Marxism and the Enlightenment project manifested itself was as an outbreak of nihilistic philosophy in the early 1970s, which seemed to take Nietzsche rather than Marx as its model. *LE* (1974) belongs to this outbreak, which can also name Gilles Deleuze and Felix Guattari's *Anti-Oedipus* (1972) and Jean Baudrillard's *Symbolic Exchange and Death* (1976) amongst its products. Works such as these constitute something of a philosophical 'dead-end' as far as later commentators like Peter Dews are concerned,[6] but collectively they signal an unequivocal break with the world of well-ordered systems of thought like structuralism and Marxism, and usher in an era of iconoclastically inclined philosophical enquiry, where the desire for an apocalyptic 'revaluation of all values' on the Nietzschean model appears to be the dominant motivation.

Postmodernism carries this revaluation of all values to the logical extreme of rejecting all large-scale systems of thought – Marxism and structuralism not surprisingly being prime examples – and Lyotard gives the lead here in his seminal study *The Postmodern Condition*, with its celebrated attack on grand narratives. Lyotard seemed to sum up a generalized cultural unease in this book, which has taken on something like canonical status amongst the postmodern movement since its publication in 1979. Alongside poststructuralism, postmodernism has dominated the theoretical landscape throughout the 1980s and 1990s, and Lyotard is a crucial figure in the radical shift away from universal theories during this period (a shift mirrored in the socio-political domain by the collapse of Communist hegemony in the Soviet Union and Eastern Europe). Postmodernism is a difficult movement to define with any great degree of precision, and in fact it covers a wide spectrum of views from a rejection of tradition to an ironic reworking of older styles and ideas, but what all its adherents do seem to share is the mistrust of metanarratives that comes through so strongly in Lyotard's work from the early 1970s onwards. It is against this background of cultural crisis, where universal theory is perceived to be a massively devalued entity, and the possibility of what has been called a 'politics of redemption' (for example, Marxism) has been fatally undermined, that we must consider Lyotard's writings.

CHAPTER ONE | Lyotard's political writings

In one sense it is artificial to approach Lyotard's 'political writings' as a separate topic because this is someone who, as Geoffrey Bennington has rightly noted, is 'fundamentally a political thinker'[1] and whose entire oeuvre can be considered to have a political dimension. Nevertheless, the collection put together by Bill Readings and Kevin Paul Geiman under the title of *Political Writings* provides a useful way in to focusing on Lyotard's more overtly political works, in particular his writings on the Algerian question in the journal *Socialisme ou barbarie* during the 1950s and 1960s. In the case of the latter we can test just how 'extreme' the critique of Marxism from within was prepared to be. This chapter accordingly will range over the material presented in the Readings–Geiman collection, particularly the Algerian writings and Lyotard's thoughts on the 1968 *événements*. It will close by looking at *Heidegger and 'the jews'*, one of the most significant of Lyotard's later interventions into political debate, this time into the highly emotive 'Heidegger affair' of the late 1980s.

The Algerian Writings

Lyotard assumed responsibility for *Socialisme ou barbarie*'s Algerian section in 1955, and his writings on Algeria cover the period

1

from the mid-1950s until the declaration of a sovereign Algerian state in 1962, an event which Lyotard views with a considerable degree of unease:

> This country is still not the dwelling place of those who inhabit it; it remains to be conquered. *Some crises* may shake it, may provoke famine, unemployment, misery, despair. But none of them will be decisive, and none will bring a response to *the crisis* from which Algeria suffers, until a social class or a strongly organized and implanted section of society builds a model of new social relations and makes everyone accept it.[2]

The notably sceptical attitude towards what was elsewhere on the left being hailed as the successful outcome of a war of liberation, pervades Lyotard's writings on Algeria for *Socialisme ou barbarie*. Even in his earliest pieces on the topic he is worrying about whether the struggle that is taking place merely forms the prelude to a new kind of exploitation of the North African peoples, and arguing that Algeria calls for a rethink of the Marxist analysis of colonialism. In an era when Marxist thinkers were only too prone to force reality to be what their theory said it should be, Lyotard's is a refreshingly honest voice to encounter (and indeed that honesty is a hallmark of his career).

Throughout the course of these writings there is a generally dismissive tone adopted towards 'organized' Marxism, which positions Lyotard as a maverick figure on the left. In 'Algerian Contradictions Exposed' (1958), for example, he challenges standard Marxist interpretations of the Algerian situation on the grounds that they fail to address the realities of that situation, treating it as a latter-day equivalent of the Russian Revolution. Algeria, Lyotard points out, is essentially a peasant society and has yet to attain the social conditions that classical Marxism lays down as necessary for a successful revolution to be prosecuted. For a start there is not much of a proletariat for revolutionary ideas to ferment within: 'Just because 400,000 North African workers work in French factories and building sites, they do not constitute a proletarian avant garde' (p. 208). The misreading of the Algerian situation by most Marxist theoreticians runs deep, and Lyotard even questions the applicability of such a central Marxist notion as 'class struggle' to a country so different in its cultural traditions from the European models on which classical Marxism was based. Nationalism constitutes a more important factor than class in Algerian society, Lyotard maintains, and he condemns the way that Marxist class categories are imposed on this society despite its evident resistance to them:

> It is in a completely *abstract* way, that is, exclusively *economistic*, that one can speak of *a* proletariat, *a* middle class, *a* bourgeoisie in Algeria. If there is *a* peasantry, it is because it is entirely and exclusively Algerian, and it is this class that evidently constitutes the social base of the national movement, at the same time that it is the clearest expression of the radical expropriation that Algerian workers undergo as Algerians. (p. 210)

This will be a common complaint of the Lyotard of this period, that Marxist theory and empirical political reality do not correspond – and further, that the Marxist establishment is refusing to acknowledge that this is so. The eventual, postmodern, reaction to this disjunction, and all attempts to deny or disguise it, will be to stop deluding oneself and simply dispense with the theory altogether. While we do not have *quite* this level of postmodern ruthlessness on display in these Algerian pieces, we are clearly heading in that general direction. Postmodernism is embraced only after Lyotard has painstakingly catalogued Marxism's failings in a concrete political situation over a period of several years.

Lyotard's dissatisfaction at the highly abstract, as well as dogmatic, nature of official Marxism is a constant refrain of these analyses; hence his complaint that although the class struggle never yields up 'pure situations' the majority of Marxist theoreticians continue to act as if it did (p. 321). The frustration at such theoretical inflexibility and rigidity of thought is gradually pushing Lyotard into proto-postmodern positions. Thus he can speak bitterly of 'the confirmed decay of the ideology of the left', and note that, Communist dogma notwithstanding, 'the proletariat is no longer present in society as manifest political will' (pp. 269, 276), conclusions hardly likely to endear him to the Marxist establishment either in France or elsewhere. Even the residual Marxism within him that forces Lyotard to insist that 'This is not to say that the communist project has been annihilated and that the dominant class has succeeded for all time in its task of reifying the workers',

cannot prevent the implicitly postmodern conclusion from forming that 'A certain idea of politics dies in this society' (p. 276) once
you have realized the full extent of the discrepancy that obtains
between theory and reality. There is ample evidence that Lyotard
will not shy away from whatever the 'extreme consequences' of his
Socialisme ou barbarie 'critique of reality' may happen to be, and
they certainly do appear to be pushing him away from an ortho-
dox Marxist perspective. One by one the certainties of Marxist
dogma drop away as the Algerian situation unfolds in front of
Lyotard's eyes.

One of the consequences of Lyotard's style of critique is that
there can be no sacred cows: all aspects of Marxist dogma must
come under scrutiny, even such apparently sacrosanct entities as
the working class. Traditional Marxism tends to romanticize the
working class to some extent. It is regarded as the historic agent of
revolutionary change, the class that comes to recognize its exploitation at the hands of capital, and then, in collaboration with
the Communist Party, to overthrow its oppressors for the benefit
of all humanity (in other words it is the 'identical subject-object' of
history[3]). Communist parties invariably justify their actions as
being undertaken in the name of the working class, and Communist propaganda invariably idealizes the working class (think of the
heroic vision of the worker conveyed by socialist realism, for example). It is all but an article of faith for Communists to believe in
the essential goodness of the working class – unless of course that
class has been corrupted by the efforts of the agents of capitalism.
The theory of hegemony works on just such a principle as the
latter, arguing that the working class has been drawn into the
bourgeoisie's system of values by various devious means, such that
it is made to act against its own best interests. It is the theorist's
role to reveal what those best interests are such that the working
class can proceed to fulfil its historic emancipatory role.

Lyotard, however, is not prepared to be romantic about this
issue. Sensing yet another worrying disjunction between theory
and reality, he is not afraid to be critical of the actions of the
working class, in particular questioning its 'internationalism' (another article of faith amongst Communists). The French working
class, he complains, has shown scant interest in its North African
comrades in recent years. French workers may have engaged in
frequent strikes on their own behalf for improved wages and

working conditions, but never over the Algerian war. Lyotard notes a general lack of interest in such international issues amongst Western European working classes:

> when the independence of Vietnam, Tunisia, or Morocco was at stake, the French working class also did not actively struggle in order to aid the colonized peoples to reject the yoke of French imperialism. When the Mau-Mau rose up against British colonization, did the English workers intervene on their side in the struggle? And did the Dutch workers support the Indonesian movement? It must indeed be noted that solidarity between the proletariat of the old capitalist nations and the liberation movements of the young colonized nations does not appear spontaneously, because the European workers do not have an active awareness of the shared goals of the colonial nationalist struggle and of the class struggle; because the classic schema of this convergence remains abstract for them. (pp. 204–5)

Such an unsentimental view of the working class is relatively rare amongst Marxists of the period (at least in public expression). Once again Lyotard is not content to take the rhetoric at face value; it has to be subjected to empirical analysis, and if that does not support the rhetoric then he is quite prepared to say so in fairly blunt language. It is a bluntness that is even extended to cover relationships between Marxist activists, whose supposed solidarity and internationalism, when viewed closely, reveals paternalistic attitudes on the part of European militants towards their Algerian comrades.

When Lyotard examines 'The State and Politics in the France of 1960' against a colonial background of a state of siege in Algiers, he finds a sorry state of affairs: a nation that is 'politically dead' (p. 252), a depoliticized proletariat, and a discredited set of institutions on the left. Lyotard is not willing to make many excuses for this proletariat either, arguing that it has colluded in its own marginalization by the forces of capital. Reflecting on yet another French political crisis, Lyotard notes that, as well as being compromised by an often devious Communist Party, 'the proletariat left capital at leisure to resolve the crisis in its best interests. What is more, the proletariat helped in the process, first by its abstention, then by its vote in the referendum' (p. 255). It is this political apathy that has prepared the way for the Gaullist regime, and it prompts Lyotard to call into question the whole basis of Marxism as a social philosophy. What is the point of the socialist project, he wonders, if 'this project no longer exists among the proletariat'? This is dangerous territory for a Marxist to stray into, and it indicates the depth of disenchantment that Lyotard is feeling after several years of scrutinizing the relationship between theory and reality in the Algerian situation. Neither is Lyotard willing to take refuge in the traditional Marxist 'solution' to such discrepancies, that is, to continue on regardless with the theory; 'imposing out-dated political categories on this world, by applying a political practice to it that does not correspond to reality' (p. 256), goes against his revolutionary spirit. Where this refusal to compromise is leading Lyotard, it is clear, is out of the Marxist camp al-together, and by 1960 he is already on the cusp of postmodernism.

Algeria becomes for Lyotard a symbol of Marxism's lack of touch with reality: it is not just the French who are defeated in the colonial war, but Marxist theory itself. The Marxist establishment stands revealed as being in a time warp, the Algerian insurrection graphically demonstrating 'their complete inability to rethink the political problem of the modern society or of the society on the way to modernization in which they find themselves. They do nothing but chew over the old slogan of the union of the left' (p. 268). It is a familiar refrain of Lyotard's but one which is becoming ever more insistent by the 1960s, and he is beginning to draw radical conclusions from his researches into Algeria's impact on the French socialist establishment: 'Evidently, no political perspective could be outlined by the organizations of the "left," which deserve no further critical attention' (p. 269). Something of the characteristic postmodern tendency simply to opt out of debate with entrenched interests is surfacing at such points. The inex-orability of the argument, and Lyotard's creditable rejection of the standard avoidance tactics that Marxism offers to him in such situations, generates the bleak conclusion that 'A certain idea of politics dies in this society'. When Lyotard then goes on to exhort the reader that 'It is now time for revolutionaries to measure up to the revolution to be made' (p. 276), one really has to ask oneself whether he has anything particularly Marxist in mind any longer.

Another one of the 'extreme consequences' of Lyotard's critique is a suspicion concerning the motives of the leaders of the revolu-tion. As early as 1957 he is worrying about the FLN's (Algerian National Liberation Front) growing bureaucratization as a movement and the implication this holds for a future independent Algeria. The fear he expresses is that the FLN will effectively take over the state, and that the revolution's leaders will turn the revolution to their own personal advantage, as had happened in so many ex-colonial nations. Later in 'Algeria Evacuated' (1963) he is clearly hinting that this is indeed what is occurring in the new Algerian state, that it is power rather than socialist idealism that is the driving force of the Algerian political elite, and he remarks contemptuously of the leader Ben Bella's so-called 'Algerian socialism' that,

> This new variety of socialism has the original features of considering the working class as incapable of radically transforming society, of excluding workers' demands from its program, and of seeking its social base among the petite bourgeoisie and the peasantry. (p. 306)

Already in the early days of independence Lyotard can see a gap opening up between rulers and ruled, describing the relationship between Ben Bella's government and the peasant class that makes up the bulk of Algeria's population as merely 'formal' and 'plebiscitary' (p. 312). For Lyotard theory and reality are beginning to diverge yet again.

The Lyotard of the Algerian pieces and the Lyotard of postmodernism may be different people, but there are nevertheless many common features to note between his Marxist and post-Marxist phases. In the first place there is a deep mistrust – the true sceptic's mistrust we might say – of authority that runs throughout his career. In the 1950s and 1960s this mistrust manifests itself as a generalized suspicion of the motives of the Communist Party, and in fact of official Marxism in all its guises (Lyotard is not one for uncritical hero worship of the Soviet Union or Maoist China), as well as, more predictably, of the bourgeois state and its functionaries. There is a constant suspicion of almost all of those in positions of power: the Algerian revolutionary leaders no less than the figures at the top of the French Communist Party, the French trade union movement or the French government. Lyotard strikes an authentically anti-authoritarian postmodern note when he comments in 1961 that, 'For years the young have been condemned to the following choice: either play with the rattle offered by the parties under the name of politics or completely lose interest'

(p. 282). The growing tendency of young voters to refuse such a loaded choice is for Lyotard one of the most hopeful political signs around as the Algerian situation reaches its climax.

What also comes through strongly in both the Marxist and post-Marxist phases is a concern for the individual caught up in the toils of mass politics and universal theories. Lyotard's later championship of 'little narrative' over 'grand narrative' (in effect, the individual over the system) is prefigured in remarks like the following, delivered in the immediate aftermath of Algerian independence:

> the problem of helping Algerians to live is conceived and solved in terms of an individual or a small collectivity, a village, a family, a quarter. No consciousness can span the whole of society so as to pose the question of what that society is for itself. The unemployed person wants work; the woman wants bread for her son; the combatant wants to be honored for having fought; the student wants books and professors; the worker wants a salary; the peasant wants seeds; the shopkeeper wants to restart business. No one, no political group, no social class is able to build and propagate a new image of Algeria that Algeria might desire as it had desired independence. (p. 302)

There is a clear shift here away from universal theories on the Marxist model that prescribe individual behaviour, to something much more personalized. The lesson is that there is no such thing as 'the Algerian people', any more than there is 'the proletariat'. What Lyotard identifies instead is a complex of conflicting needs and desires experienced at individual level: precisely what he will go on to celebrate in his later postmodern works such as *PC*, where the 'little narrative' (individual, small collectivity, village, family, quarter) becomes the focus of attention, and the means by which 'grand narrative' is systematically to be undermined.

We can say that Lyotard evinces a general distrust of macrocosmic theories, and a sincere desire to plead the case of the individual in the face of the encroachments of such theories, more or less throughout his entire career. Scepticism is rarely far from the surface. In fact theory is almost always in the dock as far as Lyotard is concerned, always having to justify itself (as is authority in general). After a certain point – and by the end of the Algerian colonial war we are well on the way to that point – some kind of a break with classical Marxism becomes all but inevitable. In that sense Lyotard's Algerian writings can be considered to constitute important documents in the development of postmodernism.

Nanterre and the 1968 'Événements'

Given the critical role played by1968 in his intellectual develop- ment, it is worth our while exploring some of Lyotard's comments on the *événements*. Lyotard was on the staff of the University of Paris at Nanterre at the time (Nanterre being the main centre of student political activity during the *événements*), and 'Preamble to a Charter'[4] (1968) communicates the intoxicating atmosphere of the time in French university circles, the sense that, as Lyotard's unusually high-flown rhetoric has it, 'a new period of history' has been ushered in.

The document begins by staking out a socially subversive role for the university sector to fulfil:

> Our task will be that of displacing the entire institution of the university as fully as possible from the functions to which it is restricted by both the ruling class and its own deeply internalized repressions, in order to turn it into a place for working out the means of the critical understand- ing and expression of reality . . . Our task is not simply to 'make the faculty work' (for whom, to what ends?) but to criticize, to deconstruct the institution, to determine the orientation we want to give to our work, to develop a program for this work, and to realize it. (p. 41)

Once again we can see the concern to ensure that theory is address- ing itself to reality, as well as the desire to undermine the tendency towards elitism and bureaucratization of theoretically oriented in- stitutions. The growing sense of community between workers and students offers real hope to Lyotard that the elitism and bureau- cratization that had distorted the Algerian revolution can be over- come this time around, and enough of his Marxist past remains for him to view the alliance of students and workers as a possible instance of the highly desired union of theory and practice.

The anti-authoritarianism that became such a feature of the Algerian analyses emerges in Lyotard's exhortation to the Nan- terre Faculty of Letters to ensure that university reforms are not left to the powers that be and moderates within the staff and student body; rather, radicals must 'impose institutions and modes of teaching and research that allow the critical comprehension of reality in all its forms and the liberation of the power of expression' (p. 44). Behind the rhetoric lies a desire to revitalize the public life of a nation that only a few years before Lyotard had been pronouncing 'politically dead', a desire to see politics begin to function again at the level of individual, small collectivity, village, family, quarter.

Given the hopes aroused by the *événements*, the repression that swiftly followed hit Lyotard all the harder. Nanterre was the subject of police occupation for quite a long period after the *événements*, and in 'Nanterre, Here, Now'[5] (1970) Lyotard vents his anger at the heavy-handed approach taken by the authorities to restoring 'order' on campus. Lyotard can see little difference between the order sought by the authorities and that by various groups on the left – his anti-authoritarianism coming to the fore yet again. Thus we find him complaining bitterly about the appropriation of the struggle by established political groupings (the Communist Party, etc.) such that its purity of motive and originality of thought is rapidly lost:

> The same goes for political discourse: there, too, a phraseology is handed down to us and we reproduce it faithfully. We let our relation to our political activity and to our comrades be mediated by an institutionalized *form* of speech. This institution most obviously consists of placing this speech once and for all in the mouth of a great dead man: Marx or Lenin or Trotsky or Mao (he may not be dead, but he is oriental – the Bajazet of politics). Thus the symbolic Father continues, under various imaginary costumes, to govern our words and our acts; thus the question of power among our own ranks is always stifled, always displaced into the question of the power facing us. (p. 49)

'The question of power' is one that will always exercise Lyotard, and he notes with dismay (although perhaps not surprise) an eruption of infighting on the left, with Communists vilifying Maoists and Maoists all too predictably replying in kind against Communist 'revisionism', as well as collusion between certain elements of the left and the authorities. As far as Lyotard is concerned it is the usual problem of vested interests trying to protect their power base against outsiders, and in the process any possibility of real change is lost:

The real critique of the system can only take place (at least at the moment, and for the foreseeable future) through interventions of the *here and now* kind, decided on and managed by those who make it. The critique of capitalism and of its university in meetings, even if they take place in the teaching establishments, is immediately digested by the system. The organization and its discourse, even if they are revolutionary in their signified, are made of the same stuff as the objects of their criticism. (p. 57)

'The here and now kind' of political action is to become the preferred option in Lyotard's postmodern world (where it will be variously described as 'paganism' or 'svelteness'), and it cuts against the traditional Marxist demand for carefully controlled revolutionary situations that the party can direct centrally.

Most Marxist theorists would describe what Lyotard is advocating at this point as 'adventurism' or 'spontaneism', and those are serious charges within the Marxist movement (Lenin can be particularly harsh about such 'deviations' from the true faith). Lyotard's somewhat ingenuous denial of the 'spontaneist' label on the grounds that 'here and now' activism 'does not propose the seizure of power, but the destruction of powers' (p. 59), would be found singularly unconvincing by most classical Marxists, who would simply see it as further damning proof of deviationist tendencies on his part.

Lyotard has moved well into post-Marxist territory by the end of 'Nanterre, Here, Now', more or less dismissing Marxism's revolutionary credentials as a sham: 'You may say that a boycott of ticket punching in three Metro stations will not overthrow capitalism. But let's be understood: neither will the seizure of power by a large party of the Bolshevik kind' (p. 58). Marxism, it is claimed, is no more than a mirror image of capitalist repression, and in a closing gesture that reveals the depth of his frustration he calls for an 'apedagogy' to replace dialectical materialist method. Clearly, any semblance of dialogue between Lyotard and the Marxist tradition is now at an end; a commitment to apedagogy constitutes a sweeping rejection of a movement which lays so much store by political education and rational argument.

One of the key organizations on campus at Nanterre during the *événements* was the 'March 22' movement, which was formed to commemorate student protests at the arrest of several members of the National Vietnam Committee on 22 March 1968. Lyotard's essay 'March 23', subtitled an 'Unpublished Introduction to an Unfinished Book on the Movement of March 22'[6], constitutes a memorial for the movement and the ideals that had motivated it (in fact March 22 owed far less to traditional socialist thought than it did to situationism[7]).

Lyotard sets out to capture something of the *événements'* shock-value in this piece, which he is careful to differentiate from the genre of 'history'. 'The only way to excuse having written a history book on the March 22 movement', he warns,

> is for it not to be a book of history, for it not to dissolve the delirium, the unjustifiability, and the passion into a simple movement to be understood. Rather, such a book must in its turn be an *event*, an event like the displacement and reinforcement of critique of which the March 22 movement was the head and arm for a few weeks. (p. 60)

'Event' is a term with a special resonance in later Lyotard. Events have a sense of uniqueness to them which resists organizing into the neat dialectical patterns of Marxist method, where such and such a cause is taken to lead inevitably to such and such an effect, and all historical effects in their turn can be traced clearly back to specific historical causes. Rather than such causally based certainties we now have the event, seen as a force which all but overwhelms theoretical systems, being 'the impact, on the system, of floods of energy such that the system does not manage to bind and channel this energy . . . the traumatic encounter of energy with the regulating institution' (p. 64). Marxism is little more than a memory at such critical junctures, and Lyotard proceeds to reject the idea of a universal theory *per se*, insisting that, 'It is time to get rid of the illusion that universal history provides the universal tribunal, that some last judgement is prepared and fulfilled in history' (p. 67). The anti-universal, anti-judgemental 'libidinal' phase of Lyotard's career is now under way.

Heidegger and 'the jews'

Lyotard has been much exercised over his career by the Jewish question and the impossibility of ever really coming to terms with the fact of events like Auschwitz (Bill Readings speaks of a 'turn to Judaism'[8] in his later work). Addressing a Heidegger conference in 1989 he speaks of how his own study of German language and culture, maintained from his pre-war schooldays onwards, 'will always be a wounded pleasure. For half a century, this wound has borne the symbolic name of Auschwitz'.[9] *Heidegger and 'the jews'* is one of Lyotard's most sustained meditations on this 'wound', and is motivated by a desire, in the context of the 'Heidegger affair', to reach an understanding of the German philosopher's silence on the subject of Auschwitz. The 'Heidegger affair' was the product of the publication in France in 1987 of Victor Farías's *Heidegger and the Nazis*, essentially a condemnation of Heidegger as an out-and-out Nazi for most of his life. The book created a storm of controversy, hardly surprising given Heidegger's enormous influence on modern French thought, and provoked many French intellectuals to respond to this attempt to discredit Heidegger's entire philosophy on the basis of his political beliefs. As Lyotard put it, 'There is a pressing need to think the Heidegger affair', hence his intervention into this politically explosive debate.[10]

The Nazi 'final solution' to 'the Jewish question' is seen by Lyotard as a desperate project to exterminate what the Jews represent in Western thought and culture, and what they represent is the unpresentable; Auschwitz thus becomes an attempt 'to "terminate" the interminable' (p. 25). Although the Jewish people have traditionally been the target of such cultural intolerance, Lyotard remarking that 'What is most real about real Jews is that Europe, in any case, does not know what to do with them', he subsumes them within a larger category that he calls 'the jews', who represent all those marginalized by Western culture over the course of its history: nonconformist figures such as artists, anarchists, blacks and Arabs. ' "The jews" ', it is contended, 'are the object of a dismissal with which Jews, in particular, are afflicted in reality' (p. 3). The concern seems to be, as David Carroll has suggested in his Introduction to *Hj*, 'to make "jews" of all of us' (p. xii); in other words, to make us aware how vulnerable we all are as little narratives in the face of the power of ruthless and ambitious grand narratives.

For Lyotard 'the jews' are, by definition, unassimilable within Western culture in its imperialist guise (of which the Enlightenment project and capitalism can be considered latter-day expressions), and indeed resistant to its imperatives:

It seems to me, to be brief, that 'the jews' are within the 'spirit' of the
Occident that is so preoccupied with foundational thinking, what
resists this spirit; within its will, the will to want, what gets in the way
of this will . . . They are what cannot be domesticated in the obsession
to dominate, in the compulsion to control domain, in the passion for
empire, recurrent ever since Hellenistic Greece and Christian Rome.
'The jews', never at home wherever they are, cannot be integrated,
converted, or expelled. They are also always away from home when
they are at home, in their so-called own tradition, because it includes
exodus as its beginning, excision, impropriety, and respect for the
forgotten. (p. 22)

It is this 'respect for the forgotten' that signals the injustice done
to both 'the jews' and 'the Jews'; in the case of the latter, the
slaughter of the 'final solution' – in fact, their treatment
throughout almost the whole of Western history – 'pretends to be
without memory, without trace' (p. 23). What Lyotard calls 'the
politics of forgetting' takes over, with the argument being that the
unpresentable does not exist (revisionist historians denying the
fact of Auschwitz, for example), and it is in this connection that
Heidegger is held to be culpable: he 'has lent to extermination not
his hand and not even his thought but his silence and nonthought.
That he "forgot" the extermination' (p. 82).

It is not for Lyotard a question of reading off Heidegger's
politics from his philosophy, nor of trying to deny the depth of his
commitment to Nazism (the latter being 'deliberate, profound, and
in a certain way persistent'). To do either of these is to reduce the
'Heidegger affair' to a simplistic choice along the lines of 'if a great
thinker, then not a Nazi; if a Nazi, then not a great thinker – the
implication being: either negligible Nazism or negligible thought'.
It is rather a case of insisting on the fact of Heidegger's wilful
'forgetting' and what lies behind that process. As we shall go on to
see, Lyotard's vision of a philosopher is one who refuses the temp-
tations offered by the 'politics of forgetting', and who 'bears witness' to the plight of 'the jews': that is, those excluded from
discourse throughout the course of Western history. What we have
instead in Heidegger is 'a mute silence that lets nothing be heard.
A leaden silence' (p. 52). Just as thought always exceeds its particular socio-historical contexts (something that Farías's book does
not recognize, in Lyotard's view) so Heidegger's thought exceeds
Nazism, with Lyotard arguing that 'he takes, even throws himself,

furiously, much further than Nazism, well beyond and outside it'
(p. 64).

Critical to this interpretation is Heidegger's use of the term
Volk in *Being and Time,* and his notion of its 'destiny'. The second
part of the work, Lyotard notes,

> is devoted to the *power* that *Dasein*, and notably that destiny called
> *Volk*, has to escape from inauthenticity and to open itself to the
> future-as-coming toward of its fate by giving (delivering) to itself the
> knowledge of its 'having-been' – what is called *historicality*. This
> *knowledge* does not in effect give rise to a program, but certainly to an
> authentic project . . . Heideggerean 'politics' realizes, 'acts out,' a
> thought that, as written in *Sein und Zeit, permits* this politics without
> in any way necessitating it. (p. 67)

What is lost in this 'authentic project' is, precisely, the little
narratives of 'the jews', a point hammered home in some remarks
made by Heidegger at a conference in Tubingen in 1933, the year
of the Nazi takeover in Germany: 'To learn is to give yourself to
yourself – grounded in that original possession of your existence
like a member of a people [*volkisches Dasein*] and being conscious
of yourself as co-holder of the truth of the people in its state'
(quoted, p. 69). The little narrative is absorbed in the grander
project of realizing 'the people's' 'destiny', a project which permits
the 'forgetting' of any 'jews' who refuse to recognize 'the truth of
the people in its state': in effect, the extermination of the unpresentable. The tragedy of 'the Jews' is the lengths to which this
'forgetting' will go under the Nazi regime.

What *Hj* does is to establish the political implications of
Heidegger's act of 'forgetting', signalled by its leaden silence and
nonthought, and to make us all aware of our vulnerability, as
'jews', before totalizing narratives, such as those which speak of
'the truth of the people' and thus close off the openness of the
future. Once again we can see the deeply political nature of
Lyotard's thought revealing itself. The relationship between
philosophy and politics is never a straightforward one to Lyotard,
but it is also never one he shies away from trying to present to us.

CHAPTER TWO

Libidinal Economy *and* the break with Marxism

Libidinal Economy put the seal on Lyotard's break with Marxism. This 'evil book, the book of evilness that everyone writing and thinking is tempted to do',[1] as he later termed it, has about it the air of a thinker at the end of his tether and it succeeded in losing Lyotard many friends on the left in France, including several of his ex-colleagues in *Socialisme ou barbarie*. Although to date it has generated surprisingly little critical response for such a philosophically provocative and confrontational work (its translator Iain Hamilton Grant noting that it is generally viewed as an example of the 'somewhat naive anti-philosophical expressionism' of the early 1970s[2]), it deserves to be regarded as one of the most remarkable documents of postmodernism, a document whose shrill and hectoring tone is in striking contrast to the studied coolness of so much later Lyotard. If we want to observe postmodernism as it is 'felt on the pulses' or 'red in tooth and claw', then *LE* is the place to go (Lyotard is later to speak of 'the upheaval it required of my soul' (*Per*, p. 13)). Many of the ideas behind the notion of 'libidinal economy' were introduced in the slightly earlier work *Discours, figure* (with *Anti-Oedipus* another likely source of influence), but it is in *LE* that the full political implications of the notion are realized.

One of the reasons that *LE* has had so little critical response in the English-speaking world is that it did not appear in fully translated form until 1993, by which time the shock-value of its violently anti-Marxist stance had largely disappeared.[3] In the intervening period we have seen the effective collapse of Marxism as a significant political force in Western Europe, and become quite used to the spectacle of Western, and in many cases Eastern, intellectuals deserting the theory in droves. One of the benefits of this delayed appearance is that one is able take a more detached view of the text and its often inflammatory and intemperate rhetoric (although this can still alienate even sympathetic commentators like David Carroll, for whom *LE* is a 'quite nasty, even arrogant' piece of writing[4]). It now looks less like an 'evil book' and more like a forthright setting of the agenda for the world of postmodern philosophy: the world where 'We deliver no message, we bear no truth, bring no revelation, and we do not speak for those who remain silent' (*LE*, p. 259) is an entirely characteristic, and no longer particularly iconoclastic sentiment. It also contains a devastating critique of the Marxist notion of 'false consciousness' that only now comes into its own given Marxism's recent history. If *LE*'s historical moment has passed, therefore, the work has gained considerable cultural resonance in the interim. I am going to argue that this is an extremely important book, a key document in the history of postmodernism in fact, and that the libidinization of discourse (particularly philosophical discourse) that Lyotard calls for, lies at the centre of the postmodern project.

It is worth bearing in mind the work's cultural context, and, in particular, how it fits into Lyotard's complex relationship to Marxism and the French Communist Party. The phenomena that loom largest in *LE*'s production in that respect are undoubtedly the 'Algerian Question' and the 1968 *événements*, both of which progressively erode Lyotard's faith in Marxist theory and its official French guardian, the PCF. Lyotard's intellectual trajectory is from Marxist militant to post-Marxist, and even anti-Marxist icon, the thinker who loftily dismisses Marxism's claims to continuing political or ethical authority: 'We no longer have recourse to the grand narratives – we can resort neither to the dialectic of Spirit nor even to the emancipation of humanity as a validation for postmodern scientific discourse' (*PC*, p. 60). Even in his Marxist phase, however, one can detect a sceptical edge, a presentiment of the postmodernism to come – deeply unfashionable though it may be to see such logical 'development' in a postmodern thinker. Neither his membership of *Socialisme ou barbarie* nor his writings on the Algerian Question suggest a proponent of Marxist orthodoxy, nor do pronouncements from that earlier period that 'When concepts or schemas are refuted by historical reality over a period of forty years, the task of revolutionaries is to discard them without remorse and to replace them with others that make an effective struggle possible', or 'how, in effect, is one to persevere in the socialist project if it appears that this project no longer exists among the proletariat, at least in its *political* form?' (*PW*, pp. 198, 256). It is not fanciful to regard *LE* as the logical, and in many ways predictable culmination of a couple of decades of growing disenchantment on Lyotard's part with all that Marxism stood for.

Lyotard was not the only French intellectual to become disillusioned by Marxism and its guardians in the aftermath of the Algerian war of liberation and the events of 1968, but few took such spectacular revenge on Marxism's theoretical heritage as he proceeded to do. *LE* is more than an act of revenge, however, it is also a rallying cry, and an angry one at that, for the cause of postmodernism; here we can find many of the characteristic hallmarks of postmodernism – the disdain for tradition and its grand narratives, the refusal to enter into debate with one's perceived opponents, the overwhelming sense of scepticism about current cultural values – in their most passionately voiced form. Above all this is a very passionate book: one can feel the rage and even pain that underpins it, a rage and pain not just at Marxism but at the entire cultural context that spawned the theory: in effect, at modernity and its works.

If *LE* is a book full of passion, rage and pain it is also a book full of some spectacularly impenetrable prose and opaque concepts. The extent of the difficulty we face is revealed when we turn to the translator's glossary in the English edition, where, as a case in point, 'The Libidinal Band/Skin' is glossed as follows:

> the band, which has, most importantly, neither an inside nor an outside, is most easily comparable to what Freud called the primary processes of the pulsions 'of' the psychical apparatus, and could be considered as a sort of analogical presentation of difference independent of the (secondary) orders of re-presentation in which identity, signification and reference are determined. Although the libidinal

band allows Lyotard to show what is necessarily excluded by represen-
tational thinking, it is not to be considered to be 'descriptively' true
(since the model would then collapse back into re-presentation) but as
more forceful and more interesting and more inventive than previous
totalizations of 'the real'. As a kind of persuasive fiction, the various
descriptions of the band wish, nevertheless, to account for the closures
and exclusions inherent to re-presentational thinking and suggest a
'pagan' manner of affirming the differences and singularities that run
through the libidinal band in an aleatory and indeterminate fashion.
(p. xii)

Most readers are likely to feel quite alienated at this point, and
wonder if the gloss is so impenetrable, what on earth will the real
thing be like? The 'Bar', the 'Great Zero', the 'Tensor', the 'Great
Ephemeral Skin', the 'Concentratory Zero', etc., are all glossed in
similarly forbidding fashion. The editor is clearly hypersensitive to
charges of trivializing the material (we have been here before in the
various 'introductions' to the classics of deconstruction, where we
are repeatedly told by assorted editors and translators how poorly
language captures the richness and complexity of the concepts in
question), and the effect of his mode of approach is to keep the
book at the level of a secret discourse serving a cult. Any attempt
at simplification is to be regarded as a sin against the integrity of
the material. This does a disservice to Lyotard and the cause of
postmodernism, and we really need to get beyond the jargon to the
emotional turmoil underpinning the work if we are to reveal its
importance in the history of recent theory. A more productive way
of dealing with *LE* might be to chance the 'sin' of simplification; to
range over the surface of the work examining the resonances of its
call for a libidinization of discourse and see where these take us.

LE boasts one of the most arresting opening sentences that you
are likely to find in a work of philosophy:

Open the so-called body and spread out all its surfaces: not only the
skin with each of its folds, wrinkles, scars, with its great velvety
planes, and contiguous to that, the scalp and its mane of hair, the
tender pubic fur, nipples, nails, hard transparent skin under the heel,
the light frills of the eyelids, set with lashes – but open and spread,
expose the labia majora, so also the labia minora with their blue
network bathed in mucus, dilate the diaphragm of the anal sphincter,
longitudinally cut and flatten out the black conduit of the rectum,

then the colon, then the caecum, now a ribbon with its surface all striated and polluted with shit; as though your dressmaker's scissors were opening the leg of an old pair of trousers, go on, expose the small intestines' alleged interior, the jejunum, the ileum, the duodenum, or else, at the other end, undo the mouth at its corners, pull out the tongue at its most distant roots and split it, spread out the bats' wings of the palate and its damp basements, open the trachea and make it the skeleton of a boat under construction; armed with scalpels and tweezers, dismantle and lay out the bundles and bodies of the encephalon; and then the whole network of veins and arteries, intact, on an immense mattress, and then the lymphatic network, and the fine bony pieces of the wrist, the ankle, take them apart and put them end to end with all the layers of nerve tissue which surround the aqueous humours and the cavernous body of the penis, and extract the great muscles, the great dorsal nets, spread them out like smooth sleeping dolphins. (p. 1)

The startling image of dissection is continued, to inform us that 'we must go immediately to the very limits of cruelty, perform the dissection of polymorphous perversion, spread out the immense membrane of the libidinal "body"' (p. 2). A clearer signal of intent that we are moving away from the world of rational explanation associated with the Enlightenment project could hardly be given. Having performed such a brutal act of dissection what are we left with? Effectively with the body as a site of libidinal *forces* – and the idea of force saturates this work; force as that which we cannot understand, cannot explain, can only experience, that complex of energies that works unbidden through us. This is not an anatomy that explains away the mystery of things, rather an anatomy that reveals the site of mysterious forces: the various forces of desire to which Freud had earlier drawn our attention. The libidinal gesture that Lyotard is making is an anti-explanatory gesture; all we can do when confronted by libidinal forces is, in the author's later words, to 'bear witness' to their inexplicability. Lyotard's subsequent obsession with 'the sublime', another phenomenon to which we can only bear witness rather than seek to control, is clearly prefigured in *LE*.

The injunction to bear witness distances Lyotard from Freudian analysis, which, ultimately, is concerned to reach a greater understanding of what lies behind, and motivates, our conscious behaviour. As Lyotard warns us, 'It is precisely *not* a matter of

analysing . . . there is *no analysis*: not even Freud's' (pp. 258, 259).
In *LE*'s terms of reference Freud still remains something of a
prisoner of the Enlightenment project and its desire to reduce
phenomena to order and understanding. While conceding that
Freudian analysis is analogous to his own project, Lyotard, following on from Deleuze and Guattari, chooses to emphasize the
darker side of force and desire, those aspects which escape analysis
and the reach of reason. Awe or respect is the more appropriate
response to libidinal force in Lyotard's universe. Lyotard had
already engaged with Freud in *Discours, figure*, where he examined
his theory of the 'dream-work', this being 'not the language of
desire, but its work'.[5] Desire is not something which can be sys-
tematized, in other words (as Lacan had claimed in his remark that
the unconscious was structured like a language), but a force at
loose within discourse. 'The dream-work is not a language', therefore, 'it is the effect on language of the force exerted by the figural
(as image or as form)' (*LR*, p. 51). *DF* sets up the figural (heavily
identified, as here in the case of the dream-work, with the visual)
against the discursive (writing, concepts, reason), with the former
representing an ever-present threat of disorder within the latter.

Libidinal economy is set up as a counter to political economy
(we can see Marx looming up on the horizon already), rather as
figure is set against discourse. The libidinal economist reveals to us
the site of forces and desires (the figural) – and can go no further
than that; whereas political economy holds out the promise of
explaining, even harnessing, these forces. In contrast to Marxism's
dialectical explanation of economic exploitation and class struggle,
we have instead Lyotard's highly provocative 'libidinal' anatom-
ization of the same historical process:

> look at the English proletariat, at what capital, that is to say *their
> labour*, has done to their body. You will tell me, however, that it was
> that or die. *But it was always that or die* . . . Death is not an alternative
> to it, it is a part of it, it attests to the fact that there is *jouissance* in it,
> the English unemployed did not become workers to survive, they –
> hang on tight and spit on me – *enjoyed* [*ils ont joui de*] the hysterical,
> masochistic, whatever exhaustion it was of *hanging on* in the mines, in
> the foundries, in the factories in hell, they enjoyed it, enjoyed the mass
> destruction of their organic body which was indeed imposed upon
> them, they enjoyed the decomposition of their personal identity, the
> identity that the peasant tradition had constructed for them, enjoyed

the dissolution of their families and villages, and enjoyed the new monstrous *anonymity* of the suburbs and the pubs in the morning and evening. (*LE*, p. 111)

In other words, libidinal forces were working through these groups, it was not a case of false consciousness, of the workers having been misled by the establishment-biased ideology of the time. At such points the text really does resonate for a 1990s audience. Standard left-wing analyses would explain away the triumph of the right and unfettered market economics in Western society in the last couple of decades as a case of most people failing, for one reason or another (ideological hegemony, etc.), to recognize where their own best interests really lay. A Lyotardean analysis, on the other hand, would argue that countries with a right-wing government, far from being in the grip of a collective ideological delusion, are in fact getting exactly what they want politically; that countries with high unemployment figures must want to be in that condition; that countries who are ravaged by war must want that to be the case too. If there is any delusion around it is on the part of left-wing political economists who think that false consciousness is an adequate explanation of human behaviour. (It should be noted that even as a Marxist Lyotard was wary of the notion of false consciousness: 'We have to get rid of a certain kind of patronizing Marxism', he had written in 1958 in one of his Algerian pieces, 'an ideology has no less *reality* (even and above all if it is *false*) than the objective relations to which this Marxism wants to reduce it' (*PW*, p. 199)). Libidinal force, Lyotard is contending, simply escapes the 'false consciousness' reading.

If Lyotard is right about the shortcomings of false consciousness as an explanatory device, then the consequences for the left are fairly devastating. Libidinal economy drives a wedge between theory and practice – whose conjunction is exactly what all Marxists are seeking to achieve – to the extent of seeming to demonstrate the *impossibility* of any effective political practice at all (for Peter Dews, for example, *LE* is 'a text bereft of any political or moral orientation'[6]). Where the left would go from there, it is not at all clear: where the erstwhile Marxist Lyotard goes is unapologetically into the rejection of the entire apparatus of Marxist theory.

Undoubtedly the centrepiece of *LE* is the attack on Marx and Marxism in the chapter entitled 'The Desire Named Marx'. Lyotard is writing from within a cultural context in which the search for the 'true' Marx is still being conducted – if not perhaps with quite the same fervour as in pre-1968 days. This is the era, or only just past it anyway, of the debate as to what constitutes the 'right' reading of Marx, and where Althusser's structuralist-inclined revision of Marxism is still a very powerful force within French intellectual circles. For Althusserians the right reading is the one that privileges the Marx of the *German Ideology* onwards, the Marx who makes the decisive 'epistemological break' between his early proto-Hegelian thought and writings and the scientific Marxism of his later career. Above all this is a *rational* and a *scientific* Marx (in the old positive sense of 'scientific').

Into this context, rather in the manner of a bombshell, comes *LE*. There are certainly no 'right' readings on offer here:

> We no longer want to correct Marx, to reread him or to read him in the sense that the little Althusserians would like to 'read *Capital*': to interpret it according to 'its truth'. We have no plan to be true, to give the truth of Marx . . . Let's repeat it over and again, we are not going to do a critique of Marx. (pp. 96, 103)

Instead of critique we are offered the libidinization of Marx – 'we wonder what there is of the libido in Marx' (p. 96) – and in some sense the libidinization of all Enlightenment philosophy. Marx is to be treated as a symbol of Enlightenment philosophy's pretensions, as well as its underlying contradictions and failings: 'We must come to take Marx as if he were a writer, an author full of affects, take his text as a madness and not as a theory' (p. 95). Lyotard therefore places himself in direct confrontation with the Marxist establishment, those 'paranoiacs' and 'Whites of the left' (p. 96) as he contemptuously refers to them. What the paranoiacs cannot cope with is, precisely, libido: the uncontrolled, the uncontrollable, the *excess* of energy, drives and production. And excess, as Lyotard almost gleefully notes, is exactly what capitalism specializes in.

Marx himself is seen to be a victim of libido's operation; as Lyotard provocatively points out, there is no closure to be found in Marx's work, which is a somewhat sprawling mess of unfinished manuscripts (eventually to be 'tidied up' by Engels). Dialectical method is, in Marx's own case, a generator of linguistic excess rather than any order or design; thus we have what to Lyotard is an astonishing aspect of Marx's career:

> the perpetual *postponement* of finishing work on *Capital*, a chapter becoming a book, a section a chapter, a paragraph a section, by a process of cancerization of theoretical discourse, by a totally pulsional proliferation of a network of concepts hitherto destined on the contrary to 'finalize', to 'define' and to justify a proletarian politics . . . for Marx (and therefore for Engels the impatient!), it must rather have been a bizarre, worrying fact. (pp. 96–7)

We are left, Lyotard argues, with 'the desire named Marx' rather than the more usual picture of the 'system named Marx' (or perhaps more properly, 'the system named Marx-Engels').

It is a short step from here to a proletariat which embraces exploitation: in other words to the death of the notion of false consciousness, on which so much of Marxism as a social philosophy depends. To challenge false consciousness is to strike at the heart of Marxist theory, and to announce the arrival of postmodernism at its most sceptical; as Lyotard goes on to put it in his most cynical-sounding fashion, 'Why, political intellectuals, do you incline *towards* the proletariat? In commiseration for what?' (p. 115). False consciousness for Lyotard turns out to be nothing more than a misreading of the effects of libidinal force.

If we return to the book's conceptual terms, we can perhaps cut through the jargon and regard them all as terms denoting 'force', 'desire' or 'energy'. *LE* is a series of demonstrations of how that force resists closure – can *only* resist closure, political or otherwise – and of how force disrupts the best-laid political practice. 'Force', Lyotard insists, 'belongs to no-one' (p. 261); 'desire cannot be assumed, accepted, understood, locked up in names' (p. 20). If Lyotard is right, if libidinal economy really does take precedence over political economy, then theory never can be turned into practice. Theory is the realm where libidinal economy is ignored, practice the realm where libidinal economy is all-pervasive – *chaotically* all-pervasive as far as poor theory is concerned. Marx's own work constitutes an all-too-ironic example of the inability of theory to control the effects of a rampaging libidinal economy.

A similar lesson is there to be learned from recent scientific practice, where theory is continually challenged and displaced by unknown forces: '*Who knows* in today's scientific knowledge? . . . The delirious sweeping of the theoretical field by modern science not only eliminates the supposedly knowing subject, it disqualifies the supposed subject.' The ultimate effect is to leave us with a science which is less of the rationally ordered process of the Enlightenment ideal than a 'delirium assumed and carried to its end'. In a characteristically provocative image, the modern scientist becomes 'a barbarian on the agora' (p. 253). The libidinal theorist is, we must assume, a similarly barbarously inclined animal.

The libidinal gesture outlined in *LE* helps us to read later Lyotard. What he is to call our 'incredulity toward metanarratives' (*PC*, p. xxiv), derives from a recognition that libidinal economy always, and inevitably, disrupts the desired union of theory and practice. Libidinal economy is to be understood as the state which calls into question all efforts at 'grand narrative' closure, the state to which we can do no more than bear witness, as when *PC*'s Appendix, 'Answering the Question: What is Postmodernism?' directs us to 'be witnesses to the unpresentable' (p. 82). The 'unpresentable', and then the 'sublime', grow out of the notion of libidinal economy. The often magisterial tone of later Lyotard – where disdain for tradition is raised almost to an art form – needs to be viewed against the rage, pain and, as the translator of *LE* puts it, the sense of 'loathing of critique' (Introduction, p. xxiv) of the earlier work. *LE* ought to teach us that postmodernism, for all that it can appear on occasion to be an affected and superficial discourse, is in reality born of a violent reaction to theory's perceived failings.

LE can also be seen as a significant intervention in a long-running philosophical dispute about the role of the body. On the whole the body has had a bad press in the history of philosophy: one only has to think of the suspicion with which it is viewed in Plato, for example, or indeed of its utter disposability when we come to Descartes and the theory of mind–body dualism, where non-material mind is held to outlast the body. Even Marxism, that apparently most material-minded of philosophical discourses, cannot resolve the problem of the body. At base, this is a problem of power and control: Do we ever really control the body? Are we, in reality, at the mercy of the action of the libido? One of the great virtues of *LE* (as with *Anti-Oedipus*) is that it puts the body firmly back onto philosophy's agenda – the extraordinary opening paragraph alone surely achieves that – and not just the body, but the body as a site for the play of libidinal forces and the discharge of energy. Any political or social philosophy which neglects to take account of the body at the libidinal level will, Lyotard insists, ultimately fail in the real world.

The message for the left that emerges from *LE* is a bleak one, and Lyotard cannot resist rubbing salt in the wound he has created. Political economy, he suggests, 'is the "left's" illusion *par excellence*' (p. 238); there is no point in engaging in dialogue with radical socialism, when it will 'always confuse *power and force*', and be reduced to using fascism as a 'scarecrow' to ensure the suppression of libidinal forces that its socio-political theory cannot encompass (pp. 32, 31). The attack on the left is remorseless, as is the attack on all that the Enlightenment project has traditionally held dear: phenomena such as rationality, order, control and explanation. The world picture that Lyotard presents us with is one of chaos, undecidability, and resistance to any kind of human control. 'There are only encounters, each tracing at full speed around itself a multitude of transparent walls, secret thresholds, open grounds, empty skies in which each encounter flees from itself, overflows itself, is forgotten – or is repeated, ceasing to be an encounter', and 'there is nothing permanent from one encounter to another', therefore we have no right 'to subordinate anything to anything else, neither permanence to discontinuity, nor the encounter to reliability' (pp. 36, 38). The philosopher's role in all this is simply to force us to acknowledge just how much lies beyond the possibility of rational explanation:

> Imagine the universe in expansion: does it flee from terror or explode with joy? Undecidable. So it is for the emotions, these polyvalent labyrinths to which, only after the event, the semiologists and psychologists will try to attribute some sense. (p. 42)

It is just such semiologists and psychologists who, as *DF* had pointed out, insist on the primacy of discourse and try, vainly, to deny the fact of the figure that unravels their theory. The dream-work, *pace* Lacan, will only ever make sense after the event, and even that sense is an illusion.

The uncomfortable logic of such a line of argument is that we must dispense with the delusion of control we have inherited from modernity and the Enlightenment project: 'What have we to cure? I do not know exactly, but at least and first this: the disease of the will to cure' (p. 28). Ultimately what Lyotard is preaching in *LE* is the most uncompromising form of nihilism: 'Nothing comes from anything, nothing is the effect of a cause' (p. 250). We end with the bluntest possible rejection of Marx's clarion call to philosophers to seek out ways to change the world:

> What would be interesting would be to stay put, but quietly seize every chance to function as good intensity-conducting bodies. No need for declarations, manifestos, organizations, provocations, no need for *exemplary actions*. Set dissimulation to work on behalf of intensities. Invulnerable conspiracy, headless, homeless, with neither programme nor project, deploying a thousand cancerous tensors in the bodies of signs. We invent nothing, that's it, yes, yes, yes, yes. (p. 262)

A 'yes' to non-invention, and as the sentences leading up to it clearly suggest, non-*intervention* as well ('stay put . . . No need for'), is a resounding 'no' to Marxism and its ideals. The libidinal is in, the figural is in, goal-directed action according to a teleological scheme is unequivocally out.

'A Memorial of Marxism'

The attack on Marxism is continued in *PC*, although by then the theory has been absorbed within the amorphous area of discourse known as 'grand narrative'. We shall consider *PC* in more detail in Chapter 3, but another direct assault on Marxism can be found in the 'Afterword' to *Peregrinations*, 'A Memorial of Marxism: For Pierre Souyri' (originally published in the journal *L'esprit* in 1982).[7] This details Lyotard's progressive loss of faith in Marxism, and how the event created a rift, or 'differend', with his friend and colleague in *Socialisme ou barbarie*, the historian Pierre Souyri. 'A *différend*', as Lyotard emphasizes, is not simply a disagreement, but a recognition of the incommensurability of two theoretical positions: 'not a simple divergence precisely to the extent that its object cannot enter into the debate without modifying the rules of that debate' (*Per*, p. 49). In real terms this means that, from his resignation from *Socialisme ou barbarie* in 1964 onwards, Lyotard can no longer think within the terms of reference of a classical Marxist framework of ideas. Souyri, on the other hand, remains a convinced dialectical materialist, remarking of Lyotard's reasons for leaving *Socialisme ou barbarie* (as communicated to him in a resignation letter) that, 'The problems we confront are, in my eyes, neither ill-posed nor insoluble within the framework of Marxist concepts' (quoted in *Per*, p. 48). The two positions are eventually incommensurable, and no amount of dialogue will resolve that state of affairs. Lyotard's differend with Souyri becomes symbolic of his relationship to Marxism: once a differend occurs debate rapidly becomes superfluous. It is as if from that point onwards the protagonists are speaking different languages.

Marxism simply ceases to work for Lyotard, who describes himself as being beset around this stage of his career with numerous 'frightening' questions:

> What if history and thought did not need this synthesis; what if the paradoxes had to remain paradoxes, and if the equivocacy of these universals, which are also particulars, must not be sublated? What if Marxism itself were in its turn one of those particular universals which it was not even a question of going beyond – an assumption that is still too dialectical – but which it was at the very least a question of refuting in its claim to absolute universality, all the while according it a value in its own order? But then, in what order, and what is an order? (p. 50)

The differend with Marxism is irreconcilable. Lyotard finds himself unable even to frame a question concerning Marxism's legitimacy and authority as a discourse, because that would be to concede too much to the theory (rather in the way that to pose the question 'Does God exist?' concedes too much to the opponent who is a believer). After a certain point of doubt dialogue becomes impossible, and the need for the leap into the postmodern unknown becomes imperative: 'It was not a question, for me, of refuting theses, of rejecting a doctrine, of promoting another more plausible one, but rather of leaving free and floating the relation to that Marxism' (p. 54). Marxism thenceforth declines from universal theory to one of a plurality of incommensurable discourses, which in real terms have nothing to say to each other.

A memorial of Marxism also becomes a memorial of Lyotard's past as a political militant. There is a sense of regret in the piece, regret for the intellectual certainties of a time when ' "Socialisme ou barbarie" had only one voice, and it spoke the idiom of those whom oppression habitually reduces to silence and who were then making themselves heard' (p. 68). But there is also more than a touch of the firmness of resolve of the later Lyotard, whose post-Marxist perspective, as *LE* only too graphically reveals, has been reached at considerable personal cost and who can only view the certainties of his militant past as sad delusions: the product of politically naive 'intellectuals who believed themselves to be Marxists because they read Marx and disliked bosses'. For the later, adamantly post-Marxist Lyotard, Marxist critique has failed the test of history: failed to account adequately for capitalism's 'resurrection' from the slump of the 1930s, for the rise of state monopoly capitalism in the postwar world, for the excesses of Stalinism and Maoism, or for the periodic backlashes against Communism by the Eastern European working classes in the 1950s (the East Berlin riots of 1953, or the Hungarian Uprising of 1956, for example). In each case those Western intellectuals witheringly referred to above have been unable 'to bear the revelation ideologically and even psychically' (p. 67), with the consequence that Marxist theory has become ever more divorced from the real world – and the real world, as the later Lyotard sees it, is a world of differends.

From such an uncompromisingly post-Marxist perspective, nothing remains but to offer a memorial for the dead theory, even if that unfortunately involves calling into question the entire life's work of an old friend and valued ex-colleague like Pierre Souyri, not to mention one's own past. With his characteristic sense of honesty and integrity, Lyotard does not flinch from the obligation.

CHAPTER THREE | The Postmodern Condition *and the cult of postmodernism*

The Postmodern Condition: A Report on Knowledge has turned into one of those texts that takes on a life of its own and becomes a general cultural phenomenon. Published in 1979, and translated into English as late as 1984, it has already achieved the status of 'classic' text. If we are to speak of a 'cult' of postmodernism, then *PC* would most likely qualify as its 'bible', a work almost endlessly pored over, and just as endlessly cited by an army of commentators: no study of postmodernism is complete without its references to *PC* it would seem. Lyotard's followers often like to claim that *PC* is one of its author's least representative texts, but it is the one on which Lyotard's wider reputation currently rests, and on those grounds alone it deserves careful attention in a study of this nature. It can also be argued that, far from being as unrepresentative as some would have us believe, *PC* crystallizes, in relatively accessible form, most of Lyotard's recurrent concerns: the limitations of theory, the moral bankruptcy of authority, the confusion of power and force, the unequal relationship between individual and system, to name the most prominent. This chapter will argue that latter line.

As its subtitle indicates *PC* is a book concerned in the widest sense with the role and status of knowledge in the world today, in particular with the processes by which knowledge is legitimated.

Lyotard's report, commissioned by the Conseil des Universités of the government of Quebec, ranges through science, technology and the arts to make its point that we have now entered an era where there is a crisis of legitimation. For a variety of cultural reasons which Lyotard goes on to identify, the universal theories (or as he calls them 'metanarratives' or 'grand narratives') of the past can no longer be relied upon to provide the necessary foundations for discourse, and at that point we find ourselves in 'the postmodern condition'. *PC* proceeds to examine the dilemmas posed by the postmodern condition and its legitimation crisis, and also to suggest new methods of dealing with these. The English translation of the book also includes as an appendix, 'Answering the Question: What is Postmodernism?',[1] which will be considered separately after the findings of the main 'report'.

Lyotard begins by discriminating sharply between the modern and the postmodern, and what mainly differentiates them is their attitude towards, and use of, grand narrative:

> I will use the term *modern* to designate any science that legitimates itself with reference to a metadiscourse of this kind making an explicit appeal to some grand narrative, such as the dialectics of Spirit, the hermeneutics of meaning, the emancipation of the rational or working subject, or the creation of wealth . . . I define *postmodern* as incredulity towards metanarratives.[2]

Postmodernism, as can be seen here, is more of an attitude than a theory in the older sense of the term. To be modern is to have a universal theory to which one can ultimately appeal; thus in the case of Marxism one can trace its political prescriptions – the need for class struggle, or the desirability of the dictatorship of the proletariat, for example – back to its metadiscourse of dialectical materialism, which in its turn depends on a particular reading by Marx of Hegel's 'dialectics of Spirit', where a certain process is being worked out through history to its logical conclusion: the self-realization of the 'World Spirit'. The narrative of the 'World Spirit', adapted in a particular way, is what guarantees the validity of Marxism's political prescriptions. Postmodernism hardly involves debate with the principles of this set of interlocking theories: it is simply the cessation of belief in them. To enter into debate would be, as Lyotard had noted about Marxism even during his Algerian writings, to concede too much to the enemy. One does not debate with the enemy's grand narrative, one shakes one's head at it – and then just ignores it as if the struggle against it had long since ceased to have any point: 'We no longer have recourse to the grand narratives' (p. 60).

Knowledge and its Field

Lyotard takes it as his working hypothesis that the status of knowledge alters qualitatively when we move into a postindustrial and postmodern age. The key to that alteration is the technological revolution that has occurred in recent decades, most particularly the rapid advances made in computer technology and information processing. Lyotard points out that technological transformations now dictate the form that knowledge must take in the same way that advancements in transportation systems and the media did in the past. The requirement of a postindustrial–postmodern age is that knowledge has to be translatable into information, and Lyotard predicts that as a result 'anything in the constituted body of knowledge that is not translatable in this way will be abandoned and that the direction of new research will be dictated by the possibility of its eventual results being translatable into computer language' (p. 4). This close correlation of knowledge and information processing proves to have important political repercussions that Lyotard is at pains to bring out in his presentation of the postmodern condition.

The crucial point for Lyotard is that knowledge is now a product for sale, and as such it has become a political issue. Knowledge is to be regarded as deeply implicated in the power-games of modern international politics: 'Knowledge in the form of an informational commodity indispensable to productive power is already and will continue to be, a major – perhaps *the* major – stake in the worldwide competition for power.' The consequences of such a state of affairs are far-reaching in terms of the international political order: 'It is conceivable that the nation-states will one day fight for control of information', Lyotard speculates, 'just as they battled in the past for control over territory, and afterwards for control of access to and exploitation of raw materials and cheap labour' (p. 5). Knowledge, in other words, will become an increasingly contested terrain, and the question of access to it – which in the world of advanced, and remorselessly advancing, technology is inevitably an economic issue – becomes one of the key political problems of the age. Above all, knowledge is now a question of *control*. Whichever body controls the production of knowledge gains significant political leverage: indeed, 'knowledge and power' are to be regarded as 'simply two sides of the same question', and that question is, 'who decides what knowledge is, and who knows what needs to be decided?' (pp. 8–9).

Lyotard's reflex anti-authoritarianism prompts him to postulate a typically radical solution to the problem: 'give the public free access to the memory and data banks' (p. 67); in that way, he suggests, we can prevent knowledge-production from being used for ulterior political motives by either governments or multinational corporations. In recent years the advent of the 'Internet' and the 'Information Superhighway' have held out the promise of just such free access (subject, of course, to certain basic economic conditions being met), but the openness of such systems is currently the subject of much debate, and it seems increasingly likely that some degree of governmental control – the kind of authority Lyotard so despises – eventually will be introduced.

Opening the data banks to the general public is very much an idealistic notion, therefore, and in real terms the production of knowledge is zealously controlled by a politico–economic elite of governments and multinational corporations. One only has to look at the domain of science to see the truth of this contention. Scientific research, the producer of most of today's knowledge, is, as Lyotard reminds us, arguably more under the domination of the powers-that-be than at any point in history. Whoever controls scientific research (and that means whoever has the *money* to control scientific research), effectively controls knowledge; it is a case of,

> No money, no proof – and that means no verification of statements and no truth. The games of scientific language become the games of the rich, in which whoever is the wealthiest has the best chance of being right. (p. 45)

Lyotard's dislike of authority comes through particularly strongly on this issue, and he deplores a situation where 'Scientists, technicians, and instruments are purchased not to find truth, but to augment power' (p. 46). When knowledge and power form this kind of alliance the result is all too predictable; research comes to be judged almost solely by its economic potential, and what does not have economic potential simply does not get funding.

Science, as we shall see, does have a way of getting its own back (particularly *postmodern* science), but Lyotard notes a highly instrumental attitude towards knowledge developing in the wake of the 'economic potential' criterion:

> The question (overt or implied) now asked by the professionalist student, the State, or institution of higher education is no longer 'Is it true?' but 'What use is it?' In the context of the mercantilization of knowledge, more often than not this question is equivalent to: 'Is it saleable?' (p. 51)

While old-style humanists will no doubt see this as a worrying trend (in effect, a dehumanization of learning), Lyotard manages to put a postmodern spin on it by pointing out the career opportunities that the rapid expansion of knowledge-production offers to individuals with the necessary operational skills; those who can process and manipulate knowledge are clearly in a powerful bargaining position. The full advantage will only be gained, of course, where free access to the data banks (the postmodern world's encyclopaedia, as Lyotard conceives of them) is a real possibility, hence his demand for an immediate break-up of the old monopolies for the control and dissemination of knowledge.

Knowledge for Lyotard, therefore, has become the terrain on which the conflict between modernity and postmodernity is most keenly contested – and that conflict between modernity and postmodernity is essentially one between grand narrative and little narrative.

Grand Narrative and the Legitimation Problem

Modernity is marked, in Lyotard's view, by a dependence on universal theories which serve as guarantors of 'truth'; to consider the notion that all history is the history of class struggle, for example, is to refer back to dialectical materialism and ultimately to the Hegelian 'narrative' of the dialectics of Spirit. One of the major objectives of *PC* is to undermine the claims of such theories, or grand narratives/metanarratives, and to establish the counter-claims of other kinds of narrative knowledge which circumvent, in pragmatic fashion, the legitimation problems thrown up by grand narratives. In this way Lyotard answers the question he poses himself in the Introduction to *PC*: 'Where, after the metanarratives, can legitimacy reside?' (pp. xxiv–xxv). Lyotardean postmodernism, as we shall go on to see, is scornful of the foundationalist pretensions of grand narrative discourses and feels that in every case a problem of legitimation inevitably arises: what legitimates the grand narrative itself? No grand narrative, he contends not unreasonably (this is an age-old philosophical dilemma), can provide a satisfactory answer to this question.

Lyotard examines two major forms of grand narrative legitimation, the 'narrative of emancipation' (political) and the 'speculative narrative' (philosophical), in order to demonstrate their gaps and failings. Each of these two narratives has had a critical role to play in the development of knowledge and its institutions in the modern era. In the former case we have 'humanity as the hero of liberty', who has to be rescued from the ranks of 'priests and tyrants' (p. 31) who have been preventing his access to scientific knowledge. Lyotard is scathing of the way that this narrative has been abused by the authorities in post-revolution France to justify turning higher education into little more than a nursery for the production of the state's administrative and professional officers. Thus we have the situation where, 'The State resorts to the narrative of freedom every time it assumes direct control over the training of the "people," under the name of the "nation," in order to point them down the path of progress' (p. 32). The ultimate irony of this narrative is that although ostensibly it is motivated by a desire to free humanity, in practice it involves a large degree of subordination of the individual to the state in the name of just that freedom. What is so often conveniently overlooked is that the state derives its legitimacy from the people and is not self-legitimating. Although Lyotard concentrates on the French experience to illustrate how narratives can be hijacked by interested parties to their own advantage (by now an almost obsessive theme in his work), it is clear that it would also apply in large part to Marxism, with its desire to free mankind from the yoke of capitalism so often leading to a totalitarian form of state control over the individual's behaviour (Soviet Russia or Communist China being obvious examples to name).

Lyotard locates the source of the second, speculative, kind of narrative in the debate over the founding of the University of Berlin in the early nineteenth century. What was being decided in this instance was the proper role of the university in the production of knowledge, and eventually this was established to be speculative, or philosophical, with philosophy being the means by which unity would be restored to learning. Hegel's work becomes a practical illustration of this new speculative mode, with his *Encyclopedia* (1817–27) being a notable attempt to accomplish the 'project of totalization' that the new narrative went on to demand of its adherents. Ultimately what this speculative philosophy entails is that 'knowledge first finds legitimacy within itself, and it is knowledge that is entitled to say what the State and what Society are' (p. 34). The state and society take their place as elements within the overall framework of the metanarrative: for example, within the historical process that Hegel designates as 'the dialectics of Spirit'. Lyotard suggests that Marxism sometimes contains elements of this second kind of narrative as well as of the first, with dialectical materialism functioning in a speculative fashion (not surprisingly perhaps, given its roots in the Hegelian dialectics of Spirit).

Both these styles of grand narrative are designed to be universal in their action, and both subordinate all human behaviour and historical process to the narrative's scheme. Their decline has been signalled by the explosive growth of technologies in recent decades, 'which has shifted emphasis from the ends of action to its means' (p. 37), although Lyotard also notes seeds of that decline as early as the nineteenth century. In effect, something like a 'crisis of knowledge' is built into the very structure of modern grand narratives. The speculative narrative's system-bound nature, for example, dictates that it only accepts as knowledge statements which conform to the rules of the system, thus simultaneously legitimating itself *and* the rules of the system (or not, if you are of a sceptical turn of mind).

Lyotard manifestly *is* of a sceptical turn of mind, as the following passage clearly indicates:

Take for example the speculative statement: 'A scientific statement is knowledge if and only if it can take its place in a universal process of engendering.' The question is: Is this statement knowledge as it itself defines it? Only if it can take its place in a universal process of engendering. Which it can. All it has to do is to presuppose that such a process exists (the Life of spirit) and that it is itself an expression of that process. This presupposition, in fact, is indispensable to the speculative language game. Without it, the language of legitimation would not be legitimate; it would accompany science in a nosedive into nonsense, at least if we take idealism's word for it. (pp. 38–9)

Like the hard-edged sceptic that he is, Lyotard harps on about 'presupposition', about what systems assume in order to bring themselves into operation. Presuppositions are always fair game for the sceptic, because they call into question the system's claims to authoritative statement. Assume the existence of God, and, yes, a religion makes sense from then onwards – but the initial assumption of God's existence is precisely what is at issue. Grand narratives are seen to depend, illicitly given their own terms of reference, on presupposition, which leads ultimately to 'an internal erosion of the legitimacy principle' – especially once a sceptic such as Lyotard is let loose on that material (and one might note in that scepticism an echo of the phenomenological desire to establish a form of analysis free of presuppositions).

The alternative way to treat any such presupposition, drawing on Wittgenstein's notion of 'language games', is as the entity that 'defines the set of rules one must accept in order to play the speculative game' (p. 39); that is, to jettison the idea of the universality of the narrative in question. Lyotardean postmodernism works happily with a wide range of non-universal, as well as fundamentally incommensurable narratives, but no grand narrative theorist could so easily accept such a fall from grace into pluralism: a grand narrative cannot be just one of several competing narratives, it aspires to exclusivity. Take away the element of universality and Marxism is no longer really Marxism to its adherents; the theory's claim to *ultimate* authority is not an optional extra but a defining characteristic. Pluralism is not, and it never can be, part of the world-picture for the committed Marxist believer.

There are many other kinds of narrative than grand, however, and for Lyotard they point the way out of the legitimation dilemma that the grand version brings in its wake. Our attention is drawn to the critical role that narrative form has always performed in the domain of traditional knowledge, where no legitimation crisis arises since narrative knowledge of this kind, 'does not give priority to the question of its own legitimation and . . . it certifies itself in the pragmatics of its own transmission without having recourse to argumentation and proof' (p. 27). One might say of traditional narrative that it does not depend on any metanarrative for its status, it just simply *is*. Lyotard outlines four main properties that traditional narratives (popular stories being the particular example he picks) possess: (1) they enable societies to construct criteria of competence and evaluation; (2) they lend themselves to a wide range of language games; (3) the rules governing their narration also dictate their mode of reception; (4) they follow a regular rhythm which aids retention in the memory. In the case of (1) the relative success or failure of the narrative's hero bestows legitimacy on a culture's social institutions; in (2) the openness of the narrative form permits easy movement between various kinds of statement (such as denotative to interrogative to evaluative); in (3) there are conventionally agreed positions ('narrative posts' as Lyotard refers to them) for all participants in the narrative transmission to adopt (narrator, listener, etc.) which in some sense ground each other; in (4) the fixed rhythms of, for example, Cashinahua Indian tales (the Cashinahua being from the upper Amazon[3]), come to take on a ritual quality over time which has a particular resonance within that society (nursery rhymes being an analogue within ours).

The final effect of these properties – none of which, crucially enough, involves reference to a metanarrative – is that the narratives themselves acquire an aura of authority:

> It is hard to imagine such a culture [as the Cashinahua, for example] first isolating the post of narrator from the others in order to give it a privileged status in narrative pragmatics, then inquiring into what right the narrator (who is thus disconnected from the narratee and diegesis) might have to recount what he recounts, and finally undertaking the analysis or anamnesis of its own legitimacy. (pp. 22–3)

Traditional narrative, in other words, *needs* no metanarrative, being implicated in the workings of its culture in such a manner that questions of legitimacy never arise. A narrator in such a culture is no more than someone who has heard the tale recounted in the past and is now passing it on to new listeners in his or her turn. It is narratives, not narrators, which possess authority, and 'they are legitimated by the simple fact that they do what they do' (p. 23); which is to say that their pragmatics are clearly established and clearly understood (in fact, *internalized*) within that culture. The fixed rhythms and ritual quality noted in property four go beyond questions of justification.

Scientific knowledge, on the other hand, is trapped in the problem of legitimacy. Since it burdens itself with the requirements of proof, verification, falsification, etc., it is never the case that its narratives are 'legitimated by the simple fact that they do what they do'. Indeed, science does not conceive of its theories as being merely narratives with their own particular pragmatics of reception, but as something of a far higher status – as universal truths. Since narratives cannot be proved or disproved – pragmatics being more a question of whether something works well or not than of relative truth-value – the scientist consigns them to a lower order of human activity than knowledge: 'He classifies them as belonging to a different mentality: savage, primitive, underdeveloped, backward, alienated, composed of opinions, customs, authority, prejudice, ignorance, ideology' (p. 27). The attitude of the scientist to the narrator is for Lyotard yet another example of the cultural imperialism that lies at the heart of Western civilization (and it also looks very much like yet another instalment of the age-old 'quarrel between philosophy and poetry' that stretches back at least to Plato[4]). In this respect legitimation has an important political dimension. Such unequal relationships can only be maintained, however, if the supposedly superior partner has a functioning metanarrative to bolster his or her assumption of superiority – and it is precisely the possibility of this that Lyotard is calling into question.

Lyotard's position is that science is just as much a set of narratives as any other discourse, but that it is refusing to acknowledge this in order to maintain its culturally superior position (yet another of the disjunctions between theory and reality Lyotard is so adept at identifying). Science is treated as a language game, no different in this respect from the traditional narrative game of the Cashinahua. Within science itself we can find both the research game and the teaching game. The former is a matter of proving things according to the rules of the theory – 'Not: I can prove something because reality is the way I say it is. But: as long as I can produce proof, it is permissible to think that reality is the way I say it is' (p. 24) – the latter of transmitting such 'proved' material to students as indisputable truths. As Lyotard points out, what we have in such cases is not so much proof as *adequation* (between theory and experimental results), but of course science cannot admit to this without severely damaging its cultural status in the process. He also points out just how much science has relied on narrative over the years. The 'Platonic discourse that inaugurates science is not scientific, precisely to the extent that it attempts to legitimate science' (p. 29) through the medium of narrative. By deploying narrative as the basis of its authority, Platonic discourse effectively falls into the trap of begging the question: it has to presuppose the validity of narrative knowledge to make its points, but that, of course, is what it is seeking to undermine. Descartes too, in his 'scientific' analysis of human ontology in the *Meditations on First Philosophy*, has to fall back on what has been called 'the story of a mind'.

Ultimately the charge against science is that it cannot meet its own conditions of proof. In effect it remains haunted by the question: 'What I say is true because I prove that it is – but what proof is there that my proof is true?' (p. 24). All 'solutions' to this dilemma owe far more to pragmatics than they can ever safely admit. In Lyotard's reading of its history, science is a narrative which tries to pretend that it is not a narrative – and when one realizes this, one has entered into the postmodern condition where the old rules no longer have any purchase to speak of.

Postmodern Science

When we come to postmodern science, however, knowledge has an entirely different status. Postmodern science is presented by Lyotard as a perpetual search for instabilities, its concern lying more with the generation of paradox than with logical proof. Lyotard draws heavily on the fields of chaos theory and catastrophe theory for this picture of the new scientific practice, asserting that,

> Postmodern science – by concerning itself with such things as undecidables, the limits of precise control, conflicts characterized by incomplete information, '*fracta*,' catastrophes, and pragmatic para-

doxes – is theorizing its own evolution as discontinuous, catastrophic, nonrectifiable, and paradoxical . . . It is producing not the known, but the unknown. (p. 60)

Both chaos theory and catastrophe theory certainly throw up many paradoxes (the simultaneous presence of chance and determinism in physical phenomena, for example), although it is a moot point whether that is their actual objective rather than just evidence of a particular barrier we have reached in our current state of knowledge (one generation's paradox being a later generation's solved problem, as is so often the case in scientific history). Lyotard, however, considers that the findings of these theories have implications that extend well beyond the domain of science. What they succeed in doing is undermining our whole notion of *system*, which strikes right at the basis of most social theory, and indeed at the project of modernity itself.

Until recently science has tended to be based on the general principle,

that physical systems, including the system of systems called the universe, follow regular patterns, with the result that their evolution traces a regular path and gives rise to 'normal' continuous functions. (p. 55)

A principle of this nature implies that systems, at least in theory, can be accurately predicted, and perhaps even controlled. 'Classical determinism', as Lyotard notes, 'continues to work within the framework of the unreachable – but conceivable – limit of the total knowledge of a system.' From the arrival of quantum mechanics and atomic physics onwards, however, this notion becomes increasingly difficult to sustain, and eventually we reach the eminently paradoxical situation where, 'It is not true that uncertainty (lack of control) decreases as accuracy goes up: it goes up as well' (p. 56). What chaos theory and catastrophe theory reveal to us is the impossibility of precise measurement or completely accurate prediction of physical phenomena – hence, in Lyotard's reading anyway, problematizing all sciences of human behaviour. What price social science, after all, if prediction goes out the window?

Lyotard cites Benoit Mandelbrot's research into fractals as evidence of our inability ever to achieve precise measurement. Fractals result when we apply ever greater levels of magnification to any surface; what we discover at these increasingly high levels of detail is a self-similar pattern to the one before: a pattern that is within the larger pattern and contains self-similar patterns within it in its turn. Presumably, this could go on to infinity.[5] In consequence one could never, as Mandelbrot has pointed out, manage accurately to measure a coastline, which would simply yield more and more to be measured as one became ever more precise in following the detail of its contours down to subatomic level.[6]

Catastrophe theory, the study of 'the discontinuities that can occur in determined phenomena, causing them to take unexpected forms' (pp. 58–9), provides yet more evidence of the general instability of the systems around us. Taking the homely example of a dog, Lyotard demonstrates how the seemingly paradoxical alliance of uncertainty and control is generated. The 'system' of a dog's behaviour, like any other, can be described as a mixture of 'state variables' (e.g. aggressiveness) and 'control variables' (e.g. anger and fear). Aggressiveness can be considered to increase in direct proportion to anger, which, at least theoretically, is a measurable quality. After a certain threshold anger expresses itself as attack, whereas the equivalent threshold with fear provokes flight. Under certain circumstances the two control variables can increase *together* such that the respective thresholds are approached simultaneously: at which point, 'the dog's behaviour becomes unpredictable, and can switch abruptly from attack to flight, and vice versa. The system is said to be unstable: the control variables are continuous, but the state variables are discontinuous' (p. 59). This simple example can be extended to much more complex systems, such as society or the economy, to suggest that our assumption of stability is little better than a fiction. 'All that exist', Lyotard dramatically pronounces, 'are "islands of determinism." Catastrophic antagonism is literally the rule' (p. 59).

Most social theorists are likely to regard this as a highly disturbing world-picture since it implies that systems are inherently unmanageable, a paradoxical mixture of chance and determinism that resists ordering, and Lyotard certainly wants us to reach just such a conclusion, claiming to have demonstrated the complete lack of scientific basis to systems theory and its proposed legitimation procedures. Modernity's vision of a physical world whose systems are progressively more responsive to human control as technology advances, lies in ruins if indeed 'Catastrophic antagonism is literally the rule' and systems theory proves to have no scientific basis at all. To recognize the limitations of theory is at the same time to recognize the limitations of modernity.

Lyotard, on the other hand, is unfazed by a vision of the world as a series of unstable systems, and he proceeds to turn this into a virtue, arguing the case for 'paralogy' as the goal of postmodern scientific practice. Paralogy involves the search for, and cultivation of, instabilities and paradoxes, and it becomes the basis of legit-imation in the new science. The point of the new science is taken to be 'the search for dissent' (p. 66), and here Lyotard un-equivocally distances himself from Jurgen Habermas and the 'con-sensus' school of social theory, with its belief,

> that humanity as a collective (universal) subject seeks its common emancipation through the regularization of the 'moves' permitted in all language games and that the legitimacy of any statement resides in its contributing to that emancipation.

Consensus has little value for Lyotard, especially when it comes, as it does in Habermas, tainted by association with the narrative of emancipation, and it is dismissed as an outmoded cultural value with which we postmodernists need no longer concern ourselves overmuch. The goal now is 'dissensus' and the prosecution of little narratives, as exemplified in such contemporary phenomena as the temporary working contract. While admitting that the temporary contract is also of benefit to the system – cheaper, more flexible, etc. – Lyotard sees it as a positive development nevertheless, and a practical demonstration of paralogy in action: 'it is not totally subordinated to the goal of the system, yet the system tolerates it' (p. 66). The delimited, non-universal, non-authoritarian little nar-rative is taken to be the face of our postmodern future; the way to correct the unequal relationship that has so long prevailed between individual and system.

Although materialist social theorists are likely to be far less sanguine about the virtues of the temporary contract than Lyotard (What about pensions? What about insecurity?), he believes it prevents the system from lapsing into authoritarianism by creating the need for a multiplicity of new 'moves' (always a healthy state of affairs in Lyotard's opinion). In this respect it functions in the manner of postmodern science, the model for systems henceforth, and its paralogical method of legitimation. Lyotard feels that having made the case for paralogy he has succeeded in sketching out 'the outline of a politics that would respect both the desire for justice and the desire for the unknown' (p. 67): what he is later (*Diff*) to define as a 'philosophical politics'.

Foundationalism and Anti-foundationalism

PC can be considered to represent a full-scale assault on the foundationalist ethic: the notion that one can find an unassailable ground for one's theory. Its thrust of argument is resolutely antifoundational in that it systematically calls into question the foundations of a whole range of grand narratives (collectively the basis for the modern nation state and modernity as a social project), as well as scientific practice up to the postmodern era and the philosophy, reaching back to Plato, that has underpinned that practice. Lyotard fits into a trend in recent French thought, of which Foucault, Derrida, Deleuze and Guattari, and Baudrillard are other prime exponents, which has chosen to take issue with foundationalist philosophy.[7] Poststructuralism and postmodernism in general have been intensely sceptical of all attempts to claim unproblematical foundations to discourse, and have repeatedly drawn our attention to the many unsubstantiated assumptions that lurk behind the scenes of even the most rigorous-seeming of our theories.

Lyotard links foundationalism to authority, and his argument appears to be that if he can call a discourse's foundations into question he has demolished its authority in turn. Thus, when Marxism's metanarrative is seen to be illicitly self-legitimating, the theory can lay no more claim to universal authority. Marxism, no less than any other grand narrative, cannot meet the conditions it states as being necessary for it to have authority, and as far as Lyotard is concerned we are justified in viewing it from then onwards with open 'incredulity', given that it has tacitly acknowledged its moral bankruptcy.

Lyotard's anti-foundationalism can be seen in the way that he shifts the debate about the value, or otherwise, of discourses from foundations to pragmatics. There are any number of pragmatic reasons why a discourse should be accepted (political, personal, etc.) and these need no foundations to continue to function. Value does become a rather arbitrary quality under such a dispensation (the criterion for a discourse being whether 'it works' or not), and not all philosophers are happy with the relativism that lies behind such an attitude. What might *not* be justified on the basis of an 'it works' criterion? Can one always trust those in charge of a little narrative to have no ulterior motives? Pragmatism solves some of the problems over how to ground a discourse, therefore, but only at the expense of creating several other, in many ways more intractable ones in the process. How does one discriminate, for example, between competing pragmatisms?; or competing little narratives?

Relativism also has the unfortunate drawback that if its arguments about the impossibility of grounding theories are taken to be true, then one can go on to query the 'truth' of relativism itself: does it assume a certain stability to language games that on the other hand it is strenuously engaged in denying? One could argue that although Lyotard is highly successful in showing what is questionable about the foundationalist ethos, anti-foundationalism is an essentially negative exercise that eventually creates as many problems for him as the discourses he is set on undermining.

Postmodernity and Agonistics

The postmodern condition for Lyotard, therefore, is a condition where we have moved beyond the need for grand narratives and are willing to operate with much more pragmatic legitimation procedures in our discourses than hitherto: willing, too, to explore the attractions of little narratives. It is a condition in which the little narrative can thrive without the constant threat of intervention by grand narratives seeking to extend their imperialist authority. (Or at least that is the ideal being sought; the rise of religious fundamentalism across the globe in the interim period since *PC* was written gives one pause for thought as to whether grand narrative is quite as moribund an entity as Lyotard would have us believe.)

Above all, the postmodern condition is one of conflict, where agonistics always applies: 'What is needed if we are to understand social relations in this manner, on whatever scale we choose, is not only a theory of communication, but a theory of games which accepts agonistics as a founding principle' (p. 16). Agonistics is a creative state to be in as far as Lyotard is concerned. It is a case of move and countermove on the part of the participants such that the game remains continually fluid and open-ended: 'That is why it is important to increase displacement in the games', Lyotard contends, 'and even to disorient it, in such a way as to make an unexpected "move" (a new statement)' (p. 16). New moves equal new opportunities for little narratives, and correspondingly less room for manoeuvre by those in positions of institutional authority: postmodernity being that state in which institutions are continually being placed under stress by agonistically inclined little narratives:

> We know today that the limits the institution imposes on potential language 'moves' are never established once and for all (even if they have been formally defined). Rather, the limits are themselves the stakes and provisional results of language strategies, within the institution and without. Examples: Does the university have a place for language experiments (poetics)? Can you tell stories in a cabinet meeting? Advocate a cause in a barracks? The answers are clear: yes, if the university opens creative workshops; yes, if the cabinet works with prospective scenarios; yes, if the limits of the old institution are displaced. (p. 17)

Postmodernism is at its most attractive at moments such as this, with its vision of a world where institutional authority and bureaucracy, the bane of so many people's lives in the twentieth century, can be constantly challenged, and where exciting games of move and countermove replace the unequal relationship of individual and system that is seemingly encoded into the ethos of modernity.[8] How realistic a vision it remains in a world of shrinking employment prospects for most of the world's population is, however, another question entirely.

'Answering the Question: "What is Postmodernism?"'

Lyotard's brief in this piece is to challenge Habermas's view of the social role of the arts, arguing that, 'What Habermas requires from the arts and the experiences they provide is, in short, to bridge the gap between cognitive, ethical, and political discourses, thus opening the way to a unity of experience' (p. 72). Not surprisingly such unity is held to be suspect by Lyotard, the champion of differends and incommensurabilities, and he sets out to dispute the point through a series of contrasts between modern and postmodern artistic practice. The ultimate answer he provides to the question posed by the piece is, 'Let us wage a war on totality; let us be witnesses to the unpresentable; let us activate the differences and save the honor of the name' (p. 82), a projected scheme of action which requires a certain amount of unpacking.

Totality, as we have seen, has been a constant target of Lyotard's, whether it presents itself in the form of a universalizing Marxist theory insensitive to actual socio-political reality (as in Algeria), or an imperialist modernity that encourages grand narratives to repress little narratives. To be in a war against it is to be engaged in the games of move and countermove outlined in *PC*; that is, to be seeking constantly to disorient and displace entrenched authority in whatever guise it may manifest itself.

The unpresentable is a feature of the modern no less than the postmodern; modern art, Lyotard argues, is concerned, 'to present the fact that the unpresentable exists. To make visible that there is something which can be conceived and which can neither be seen nor made visible: this is what is at stake in modern painting' (p. 78). Despite the awareness of the unpresentable, however, there is still a sense of nostalgia for a lost unity (which the unpresentable breaches, of course) amongst modernist artists, 'the nostalgia of the whole and the one, for the reconciliation of the concept and the sensible, of the transparent and the communicable experience' (pp. 81–2). It is as if these artists are not really facing up to the disturbing – but also liberating – consequences of the unpresentable, and taking refuge instead in 'the solace of good forms, the consensus of a taste which would make it possible to share collectively the nostalgia for the unattainable'. The postmodern involves a rejection of such solace, consensus, and nostalgia, in the search for an even deeper awareness of the unpresentable:

> A postmodern artist or writer is in the position of a philosopher: the text he writes, the work he produces are not in principle governed by

preestablished rules, and they cannot be judged according to a determining judgement, by applying familiar categories to the text or to the work. Those rules and categories are what the work of art itself is looking for. The artist and the writer, then, are working without rules in order to formulate the rules of what *will have been done*. (p. 81)

Postmodern artists and writers, therefore, work within the framework of their own little narratives, making moves and countermoves to activate differences and so stimulate further creativity. They 'bear witness' to the unpresentable rather than trying to hide from it in a false nostalgia. (The concern with the unpresentable links back to Lyotard's *Socialisme ou barbarie* analyses. His 1989 view is that the movement was guided by 'the idea that there is something within the system that it cannot, in principle, *deal with*. Something that a system must, by virtue of its nature, overlook' (*PW*, p. 166).)

Lyotard also puts forward a cyclical theory of postmodernism. When it comes to the arts, therefore, 'A work can become modern only if it is first postmodern. Postmodernism thus understood is not modernism at its end but in the nascent state, and this state is constant' (*PC*, p. 79). A consequence of this theory is that we can identify several postmodern periods in the past, with Lyotard contending here that Montaigne's essays are postmodern, and elsewhere claiming Rabelais and Laurence Sterne (amongst many other figures) for the postmodern cause.[9]

The Cult of Postmodernism

Lyotard is not the only theorist of the postmodern, but he has proved to be one of the most influential in spreading the gospel of a qualitative change to modern social existence, and the notion of a 'postmodern condition' is now well imprinted in the public mind. Postmodernism has, in fact, become something of a cult. The academic publishers' catalogues are stuffed full of studies exploring postmodernism's impact on just about any human activity you care to name, and even the popular media devote considerable time and space to it as a contemporary social phenomenon that touches almost everyone's lives in some way or other; there is what amounts to a postmodernism 'industry' in this respect. While there seems to be no universally agreed definition of what postmodernism actually is – definitions are many and various, as even a cursory trawl through the literature will reveal[10] – there does seem to be a widespread feeling abroad that something significant has happened to our culture in recent decades, and that our traditional cultural assumptions are under considerable strain as the century draws to a close.

Lyotard is a high profile figure in this paradigm shift, and he has helped to set the postmodern agenda as a self-conscious rejection of the principles that had inspired both modernity and modernism. In terms of artistic practice postmodernism has encouraged a return to older forms (although often with an attitude of irony towards these), as well as a sense of dialogue with the past. The latter is particularly marked in the field of architecture, where Charles Jencks's theory of 'double coding' (which calls for just such a dialogue to break the tyranny of modernist formalism and brutalism) has been highly influential.[11] Lyotard's sympathetic treatment of traditional narrative, which in his reading proves to have more in common with postmodernism's little narratives than with the intervening grand narratives of modernity, can be seen as an expression of that commitment to a dialogue with the past, which has as its motivation the desire to undermine the authority of modernity/modernism. In general terms we can say that the cult of postmodernism is anti-authoritarian in intent and that Lyotard provides it with some highly persuasive arguments regarding the philosophical failings of grand narrative. Lyotard is in fact one of the most philosophically rigorous of postmodernist theorists, a thinker who has reached the state of postmodern scepticism only after a thorough scrutiny of the grand narrative tradition – a scrutiny deep enough to induce the 'upheaval' of *LE*. So much of postmodern theory is made up of fashionable attitudinizing (Baudrillard comes to mind at such points with his coffee-table book musings on postmodern life[12]) that Lyotard's studies come to take on even greater importance as the philosophically heavyweight end of the postmodern theoretical enterprise. One could say that postmodernism's philosophical credibility is to a very large extent dependent on Lyotard's contributions.

CHAPTER FOUR

Judgement, justice and incommensurability: Just Gaming

One of the most critical problems that arises in a postmodern world is that of judgement. In the absence of grand narratives it is hard to see how value judgements can be grounded, and postmodernism is calling into question the very act of grounding itself. Lyotard is quite uncompromising on this issue: 'I judge. But if I am asked by what criteria do I judge, I will have no answer to give' (*JG*, p. 15). This is certainly not the kind of answer that we have come to expect of philosophers, one of whose traditional roles has been taken to be the provision of just such criteria; although, to be fair, Lyotard eventually does have an answer of sorts when he falls back on the use of pragmatics. Nevertheless, his position is an unsettling one if we wish to retain a commitment to a social justice free of personal prejudice in our politics, and the problem of justice looms very large in later Lyotard, particularly in *Just Gaming* and *The Differend*, the texts to which we turn our attention in the following two chapters.

Just Gaming is one of Lyotard's more appealing texts. It takes the form of a Platonic-style dialogue, structured over a period of seven days, with Jean-Loup Thébaud, editor of the influential French literary quarterly *L'esprit*, and the format, with its requirement to defend and elaborate upon positions under persistent questioning, enables Lyotard to present a much more human face to the audience than in any other of his works. Lyotard is probed vigorously on his position on such topics as judgement, justice, incommensurability, totality, paganism and the nature of inter-pretation, and the result is one of his more accessible works, if on occasion also one of his most provocative, as when he declares:

> It is quite clear that today a rational politics is no longer admissible. I mean by that the project of a science of politics must be abandoned. Politics is not a matter of science. Then, the only tenable position, as far as I am concerned, is one that I would call a 'politics of judgement,' a sort of 'critique of political judgement.' In other words, a politics that would admit that its realm is that of opinions . . . *I am for, I am against, yes, no.* Assent granted or denied. I think that it is this sort of feeling that is put into play by any political judgement. (*JG*, pp. 81–2)

'Opinion', 'feeling', pragmatics is rarely stated quite as baldly as this, and we might just query how far down this particular road we can go before politics collapses into aesthetic choice, in which case why not opt for fascism if the 'feeling' is right? In such cases little appears to separate aesthetic choice from personal prejudice. Lyotard does not believe he is sanctioning anything like fascism, and in fact little narratives ought to militate against such an even-tuality given that each is assumed to have its own delimited agenda and boundaries of operation. Yet it is the kind of accusa-tion to which he is very vulnerable in his open espousal of opinion and feeling. Neither of these entities has any great philosophical purchase, and Lyotard is being provocative in pushing their cause quite as blatantly as he does in *JG*.

Reflections on Libidinal Economy

The project begins with a revealing debate about the objectives of *LE*, and Thébaud will be speaking for many readers when he says of the book 'that the form of writing did not allow for any nego-tiating' (p. 3). Lyotard is quite unashamed of this, boasting that 'This book has been written in scandalous fashion. What is scan-dalous about it is that it is all rhetoric; it works entirely at the level of persuasion' (p. 4). Herein lies one of the major dilemmas of postmodernism: how does one discriminate between competing rhetorics (fascism versus socialism, for example)? The only answer that Lyotard can give is one along the lines above, '*I am for, I am against, yes, no.* Assent granted or denied', but that raises the spectre (for most philosophers anyway) of the end of dialogue and dialectic, and here too Lyotard is more than willing to agree, stating that he was striving for a poetic rather than a dialectical or pedagogical effect in *LE*. Somewhat alarmingly, he also refers to *LE* as having been written 'in the spirit of the bottle tossed into the ocean' (p. 5), which suggests a 'take it or leave it' approach to the act of writing that many will find irresponsible. Lyotard even insists that there is no great qualitative difference to be observed between theory and fiction – a line of argument with which we have become all too familiar in poststructuralist and postmodernist writing, where discourse is invariably reduced to the status of narrative driven by rhetorical strategies[1] (with even science coming into this category for Lyotard, as we saw in *PC*).

Such strategies on Lyotard's part can look like evasions to prevent questioning or challenging of his work (bottles tossed into the ocean are hardly invitations to formal dialogue), and at least initially that is how they are viewed by Thébaud, who complains that they serve to render conversation all but impossible between himself and Lyotard.[2] The first day's conversation turns into a fascinating sparring match between a reader who holds writers accountable for what they say as participants in a public discourse, and an author who denies such accountability or any duty to be publicly answerable for what he writes. Indeed, that first day proves to be a practical illustration of differends in action, or of the conflict between the 'grand narrative' consciousness (Thébaud) and its 'little narrative' counterpart (Lyotard), and it is worth dwelling on it for a moment as a representative instance of what happens when the critical establishment is confronted by postmodernism in full, and unrepentant, flow.

For Thébaud, *LE* has broken the (implicit) contract assumed to hold between the writer and reader of theory, that is, that to write a book 'presupposes that you are willing to discuss the theses, with the presupposition that is attached to any thesis, namely, that it is universalizable and that anyone can claim it as his or her own' (p. 5), and further, that the writer has a privileged relationship to his or her own text. Lyotard rejects the idea that *LE* constrains the formation of opinion or discussion of its theses, or that writing in any way grants privileged access to one's own productions:

you suppose a mastery of the author in relation to the reader. But what actually obtains in the relation constituted by these conversations? I have written books that have been sent off like bottles to the sea, you have read them . . . Insofar as what I wrote raised questions for you, you ask questions that in turn will raise questions for me: there is a permutation, an exchange of roles, in the very production of this book. (p. 6)

Between universalizable theses claimable by any reader as his or her own and bottles cast into the sea at random there is a considerable gulf, and it is the gulf that separates postmodernism from all those discourses associated with the Enlightenment project. Lyotard's line of argument is that 'universalizable' discourse, Plato being the first example he singles out, is in real terms highly manipulative,

a discourse in which each of the participants is, in principle, trying to produce statements such that the effects of these statements can be sent back to their author so that he may say: This is true, this is not true, and so on. In other words, so that he can control, or contribute to the control of, these effects. (p. 4)

One could even argue as to whether the Platonic dialogue is dialectical in the stricter sense of the term (that is, creative of new and not always predictable states of affairs), given that the conclusions of the dialogues are so heavily predetermined (in Socrates' favour usually). To throw bottles into the sea, on the other hand, is to refuse to manipulate the reader; although Thébaud has considerable difficulty in seeing it that way rather than as an instance of dereliction of a writer's duty, putting it to Lyotard that 'it is incumbent upon you, from the position of mastery that is yours, to constantly reoccupy the ground and to reorder the discourse' (p. 7) in any dialogue with a commentator such as himself. 'Mastery' is not an allowable concept in Lyotard's postmodern world of agonistic little narratives, and he is adamant that he writes for no one: 'I believe that it is important that there be no addressee' (p. 9).

A footnote (p. 6) even informs us that the initially agonistic exchange between the two men is marked by the use of the formal *vous* on Thébaud's part (as if treating Lyotard like the 'master' he refuses to be), and *tu* on Lyotard's (connoting, or at least offering, political comradeship): the clear indication being that the two are playing different, and fundamentally incommensurable, language games (Lyotard has more to gain from this than Thébaud of course).

The participants in the dialogue clash again on the vexed question of what constitutes criteria of judgement. Thébaud's strategy is to try and force Lyotard to admit that he has, at the very least, implicit criteria, even if he does try to claim that 'I judge, but if I am asked by what criteria do I judge, I will have no answer to give'. He suggests that Lyotard's work amounts to a modern version of Kant's *Critique of Judgement*, and that he is engaged in 'the working out of criteria that allows us to decide what is modern and what is not: Because you always do decide.' Lyotard's answer is a revealing one:

> Absolutely. But, to begin with, I may be wrong. Secondly, I may be the only one to hold a given opinion. Thirdly, I may change my mind about a judgement I have made. I mean that, in each instance, I have a feeling, that is all. It is a matter of feelings, however, in the sense that one can judge without concepts. (p. 15)

A matter of feeling is no small matter to the philosophical establishment if it is being allowed to function as a criterion of value judgement. Most analytical philosophers would want to argue that feelings of the kind referred to by Lyotard depend on some larger scheme of thought and are not mere reflexes or whims on the individual's part. Thébaud's rather shocked response, 'But what are you saying? I think, I find, I estimate, therefore I judge?' (p. 15), succinctly captures the disapproval of an unconverted audience to Lyotardean postmodernism's apparently arbitrary procedures of analysis. Such disapproval is hardly helped by statements of the nature: 'I have a criterion (the absence of criteria) to classify various sorts of discourse here and there' (p. 18); this is little more than mere wordplay as far as the unconverted philosopher is concerned.

The state of being in the absence of criteria is what Lyotard defines as 'paganism':

> when I speak of paganism, I am not using a concept. It is a name, neither better nor worse than others, for the denomination of a situation in which one judges without criteria. And one judges not only in matters of truth, but also in matters of beauty (of aesthetic efficacy) and in matters of justice, that is, of politics and ethics, and all without criteria. That's what I mean by paganism. (p. 16)

We shall be considering paganism in more detail in Chapter 6, but suffice to say for the time being that, although Lyotard feels he can deflect the objection, the unconverted audience will most likely argue, with Thébaud, that to be able to decide whether something qualifies as pagan or not implies at the very least a disguised criterion of judgement. Once again the gulf between postmodernism and more traditionally structured discourses yawns wide.

Justice and Pragmatics

The issue of justice is explored in more detail in the second day's proceedings, where Lyotard rejects the Platonic notion of justice and aligns himself with Aristotle (although his reading of Aristotle will be found idiosyncratic by some). The attack on Plato is essentially an attack on grand narrative and its foundational claims, Plato's idealism being one of the outstanding examples of foundationalism in Western philosophy, with its realm of forms against which all earthly phenomena are to be measured; everything in the human realm being but an imperfect copy of the perfect form located in Platonic heaven. The theory of forms stands as Plato's metanarrative and the foundation for all his other theories: social, political, epistemological, aesthetic, etc. Thus human justice is but a poor copy of the perfect justice to be found in the realm of forms. What Plato does, in Lyotard's opinion, is to assume that the theory *legitimates* the political system that he derives from it (*The Republic*'s ideal commonwealth). Marx is held to be similarly guilty of reading off the political from the theoretical, in his case the dictatorship of the proletariat from the theory of dialectical materialism:

> This type of discourse is common to an entire political tradition (that includes Marx as well), in which it is presupposed that if the denotation of the discourse that describes justice is correct, that is, if this discourse is true, then the social practice can be just insofar as it respects the distribution implied in the discourse. (p. 20)

Lyotard's objection to Plato is that justice is defined in advance of the event. An action is therefore 'just if it conforms to something defined in Plato as justice itself, that is, as the essence, or the idea, of justice' (p. 19). In common with poststructuralists like Derrida,

Lyotard takes a dim view of such essentialist thought which ex-
cludes the pragmatics he is always advocating. Effectively, justice is
referred back to the *form* of justice, which as far as Lyotard is
concerned amounts to a conflation of two different types of discourse. In Thébaud's neat summarization of the argument, 'justice
cannot be transcribed from ontology' (p. 22), these two constituting
for Lyotard incommensurable discourses. Another way of putting
this is to say that justice and truth inhabit separate language games,
that 'there is in justice, insofar as it refers to prescriptions, and it
necessarily does, a use of language that is fundamentally different
from the theoretical use'. As Lyotard somewhat maliciously notes,
the confusion of these two discourses has been used by philosophers
throughout history to claim the right to be political advisers to
rulers and governments, 'As if a good theoretical description of a
problem is what a prince needs to be able to produce correct com-
mands' (p. 24). Given the close involvement in political life of so
many French intellectuals in the postwar period (Sartre being an
outstanding example), this looks like another calculated gibe at the
pretensions of the intellectual class (the topic of intellectuals will be
considered in more detail in Chapter 9).

Lyotard coopts Aristotle into his postmodern programme by
claiming that in the *Rhetoric* and the *Nicomachean Ethics* he recognizes that justice is not a matter of conforming to predetermined
conceptual schemes, and

> that a judge worthy of his name has no true model to guide his
> judgements, and that the true nature of the judge is to pronounce
> judgements, and therefore prescriptions, just so, without criteria. This
> is, after all, what Aristotle calls prudence. It consists in dispensing
> justice without models . . . this is tantamount to stating once again
> that prescriptions are not of the order of knowledge. (p. 26)

The Aristotelian judge, in other words, does not make the characteristic mistake of the Enlightenment project of mapping the rules
of one discourse onto another, nor, it would seem, of relying on a
grand narrative at all. Thébaud's objection, which many philosophers would be quick to second, is that this is a very narrow
reading of Aristotle which leaves out of account the judge's training and education in the ways of his society, and in particular his
inculcation in the theory of the 'golden mean'. Lyotard takes the

line that the golden mean is essentially concerned with possibilities and opinions rather than truth. Further, that the mean is,

> outside of the situation in which we find it. In fact, regarding this mean, when we speak of it, we really are not saying anything that we can even conceive of, before it is determined in a concrete case. The idea of the mean is not a concept. The mean functions more like an idea, I would almost say, an idea of the understanding, than a determining concept. Unable to define once and for all, *à la* Plato, since there is no 'once and for all' here, we just have an idea to guide us. This is characteristic of the judge's position. (p. 27)

What Lyotard finds in Aristotle's notion of justice is a version of paganism, where one works, as he puts it, 'case by case' (p. 28). Judges are just not because they follow rules, but because their actions have been proved to be just – after the fact.

Postmodernism here builds a bridge back to classical empiricism, which, in Lyotard's reading of it anyway, constitutes a discourse which rejects the lure of the metanarrative (although Lyotard does concede that Aristotle's metaphysics and physics may not be as amenable to his anti-essentialist reading as the ethics prove to be). One might even see links at this point to more modern empiricist thought, as in David Hume's 'case by case' analysis of causality. Hume insisted that we could not automatically assume that a cause-and-effect sequence would fall into the same pattern as we had observed in the past, and that there was no 'necessary connexion' between cause and effect, simply what he called their 'constant conjunction'; that is, a contingent connection that could not be relied upon always to occur.[3] We could never know before the event what the pattern of cause and effect would be this time around (although we could of course *guess* on the basis of past experience). What this amounts to is a 'case by case' approach to events in the field of our sense experience, and just as Hume emphasized that no accumulation of past experience (instances of constant conjunction of cause and effect) could help us in the individual case, so Lyotard points out that past performance is no certain guide to future:

> We are not in the *always* here, but in the *often*. And therefore if the judge judges well very often, one will say that there is a presumption that she is just, but one cannot say she will always be just. Never is it always. (p. 29)

It is entirely appropriate that we can find such parallels between two of the most thoroughgoing sceptics in modern philosophical history.

A definite pattern is building up on the issue of justice, and we might see it as yet another instance of the little narrative/grand narrative division, which could be regarded as Lyotard's version of the 'particulars versus universals' debate which has been running throughout Western philosophy since the time of the Greeks. There are 'just acts', but there is no 'Justice' (this being an impeccably anti-essentialist, pro-particulars, sentiment). The former stand under no metanarrative and operate on the basis of a pragmatics, whereas the latter *necessitates* a metanarrative (as in the case of Kantian ethics, where the categorical imperative dictates precisely what action *must* be performed in a given situation regardless of whatever extenuating circumstances may happen to apply). The Aristotelian judge's pragmatics-oriented 'little narrative' can respond flexibly to events 'case by case', the Kantian judge's deontological narrative cannot (indeed, *must not*). Once again Lyotard's concern is to undermine the transcendental signified, the notion that one discourse can ever attain a position of dominance over all others. For Lyotard it is simply not possible ever to get 'outside' the field of discourse in that way (a typically poststructuralist attitude echoed by such other theorists as Derrida, for whom there is no outside 'the text'). We are forever implicated in the operation of the discourse and its pragmatics: 'We are always within opinion', as Lyotard puts it, harking back to his reading of Aristotle,

> and there is no possible discourse of truth on the situation. And there is no such discourse because one is caught up in a story, and one cannot get out of this story to take up a metalinguistic position from which the whole could be dominated. We are always immanent to stories in the making, even when we are the ones telling the story to the other. (p. 43)

To be always within opinion is to be always within a little narrative framework where pragmatics apply – and that is to be Lyotard's postmodern ideal, a world in which a multiplicity of little narratives replaces the 'terrorism' of a dominating theory concerned to extinguish the flow of opinion.

Prescriptives, Descriptives and Justice

Thébaud points out that the inability either to ground prescriptive statements or to derive them from theoretical statements, leaves us with several unanswered questions such as why prescriptive statements are kept or we feel under an obligation to be just. The questions become even more pressing, he suggests, when we realize that 'even if we do not know what it is to be just, the prescription of a "must," of an "ought" is kept'. Lyotard, on the other hand, argues that 'must' and 'ought' belong to two different languages games, and that to fail to distinguish between them is to fall into the trap of allowing theory to dominate other discourses. Both words actually mean 'must', but 'must' in two very different, incommensurable, senses, the descriptive and the prescriptive. In the former sense we have, as Lyotard puts it, ' "you must" already grafted onto an ontology' (p. 44), that is, to a discourse which already *assumes* that obligation ('you ought to do this', 'be just', etc.) *can* be deduced from a theory. It is the age-old philosophical problem of the relationship between 'ought' and 'is', with the descriptive 'is' functioning as a metanarrative in this instance since it entails a world picture, or ontology.

What we have, therefore, is yet another case of theory dictating what behaviour must be, of little narrative being dominated by imperialist grand narrative. We also have what from Lyotard's viewpoint is a classic example of the confusion that results from allowing language games to become entangled with each other, and the entanglement proves to have ideological overtones as well. Intellectuals, Lyotard informs us in one of his periodic sideswipes against this class, are only too ready to let theory dominate, to conflate language games, or to derive prescription from description, all in order 'to try to justify imperatives whatever they may be' (p. 45). *The Republic* constitutes a graphic illustration of the intellectual acting in just such a fashion as Lyotard is condemning, with notions of the ideal state being derived, ultimately, from the theory of forms such that censorship (of dramatic poets) could be justified by the imperative to maintain the state ideology at all costs. One assumes that Lyotard has in mind too the actions of the French Marxist intellectual class over the Algerian war of liberation and the 1968 *événements*, where the respective language games of political theory and political reality were forced into the same framework despite their manifest (to Lyotard anyway) differences. Whether such action is taken on behalf of a dominant or an oppositional political grouping does not affect the basic dishonesty of what is occurring, nor the culpability of the intellectuals in question in trying to further such imperatives.

Lyotard consistently plays the language game card throughout *JG*, to the point where it begins to seem all but impossible to construct an overall picture of the world. We find ourselves confronted instead by a highly fragmented universe of discrete discourses:

> I absolutely cannot put on the same plane a language game that consists in the description of reality, let us say, the game of scientific denotation (a 'reality,' we do not know what that means, but the scientist manages to make herself understood), yes, there is no common measure between such a game and, let us say, an 'artistic' language game, quite difficult to define, by the way, and of an experimental sort. Let us say Joyce, in literature. There is no common measure. (p. 50)

The lack of a common measure is what will prevent any grand narrative from ever exerting total control over the multiplicity of language games – except through the kind of theoretical violence indulged in by Platonic or Marxist intellectuals (or structuralists of the Lévi-Strauss or mid-period Barthes variety, for whom the common measure is a constant presence across discourses[4]). 'Justice', therefore, is cut off from its support system and we are left with only 'just acts', the 'just acts' of a pagan society that can still nevertheless encompass prescriptives:

> There are prescriptives in the pagan! It is fundamental, even. Just as there is a politics in the Greek city, just as there are decisions to be made by Aristotle's judge, just as the sage has to decide whether to be a father or not, to fall in love or not, and so on. There are always prescriptions; one cannot live without prescriptions . . . I believe that one of the properties of paganism is to leave prescriptions hanging, that is, they are not derived from an ontology. (p. 59)

Prescriptives at this point sound much like existential choices, with the critical difference that existential choices *do* proceed from an ontology ('being-in-itself', 'being-for-itself', 'non-being', etc.).

Existential choice minus an ontology might, in fact, be a reasonable definition of what it is like to be within a little narrative framework, although it is still possible to argue that in reality paganism amounts to a disguised ontology.

Paganism and Language Games

Lyotard's position that paganism is a state (of not having criteria) rather than a mode of being is not entirely convincing. Barry Smart has argued that Lyotard is less an advocate than an analyst of the postmodern condition,[5] in which case paganism becomes simply a description of a state of affairs that we just happen to have arrived at culturally; but it is hard to accept that Lyotard is completely neutral about this situation or that he has no stake whatsoever in it, at which point paganism becomes much more like a *preferred* state of affairs, and that is perilously close to an ontology for someone with Lyotard's anti-metanarrative outlook. When Thébaud queries where the 'specificity of paganism' (p. 60) lies, he articulates the sceptical position with regard to Lyotard's non-ontological claims for paganism.

Even if we accept the lack of any common measure, Lyotard is still open to the charge that paganism resembles a state of anarchy in which pretty much anything goes and where no language game is under a requirement to justify itself in terms of other language games. Each game seems to have its own internal justification:

> each game is played as such, which implies that it does not give itself as the game of all the other games or as the true one . . . each of these games is interesting in itself insofar as the interesting thing is to play moves. And to play moves means precisely to develop ruses, to set the imagination to work. (pp. 60–1)

Doubts begin to creep in with this idealized account of the world of language games, for all that it can sound quite attractive in its way ('imagination' invariably sends out positive signals). The picture presented looks closer to the world of sports (where there certainly is no one 'true' game) than it does to the 'games' of ethics, politics or philosophy. Whether ethics, politics or philosophy are games in the same sense as chess, is, however, another matter. Lyotard could be accused of trivializing such discourses and the problems they have to confront, and, hopefully, to resolve, by putting them in the same frame as activities such as chess: sports are not normally a matter of life and death (they are certainly not *intended* to be, anyway), whereas ethics and politics manifestly all too often are. We might just query too whether 'imagination' always has entirely positive connotations: sadists or criminals can be highly imaginative in terms of dreaming up 'moves' within their own little 'language games', but few of us would want to say that these games have no reference outside themselves or that they can in no way be judged morally. Perhaps not *every* move is a desirable move, and perhaps some moves positively cry out for some transcendental judgement to be made, whether their perpetrators find them to be 'interesting' or not.

The self-contained nature of language games is at best a mixed blessing and brings us no closer to an answer to Thébaud's searching questions. Questions about justice are invariably referred back to, and then promptly lost within the workings of, incommensurable language games, and the debate between Lyotard and Thébaud keeps coming full circle, truly a differend in action. Thébaud can only keep revealing the frustrations of the non-postmodernist by reiterating questions ('When is one unjust?', 'what do we do with a thesis like "it is unjust; I rebel"? How is one to say this if one does not know what is just and what is unjust?' (pp. 65, 66)) that postmodernism can never accept as real issues and will continue to consign, as Lyotard so deftly does, to grand narrative oblivion.

If a definition of justice is hard to come by, Lyotard does offer one of injustice. Injustice amounts to no more than being prevented from playing the game. Thus 'all terror, annihilation, massacre, etc., or their threat, are, by definition, unjust. The people whom one massacres will no longer be able to play the game of the just and the unjust' (p. 67). The only prohibition laid on a game, therefore, is not to interfere with the playing of another, but what this leaves out of account is the sheer complexity of the political game. All Lyotard can do is to keep dividing this up into a *series* of games, which is (a) certainly not how most people conceive of politics (a game of endless negotiations, compromises, temporary gains and temporary setbacks would be more like it), and (b) arguably a recipe for political quietism (just allow the government, the multinationals, etc., to get on with their own particular games, even if these do lead to a brutalizing of the society in which you live, on the understanding that they do not intervene in your own self-contained game).

Neither is it at all clear, except by process of persuasion (which does not always succeed of course), how one brings about a situation where everyone respects the injunction not to interfere with the games of others. One could accuse Lyotard of an undue amount of optimism on this score, and it is not hard to see why he has been subject to charges of providing comfort to a reactionary politics. Witness his response to a direct challenge by Thébaud to adjudicate between the prescriptions of the German government and the Red Army Fraction:

> JLT: And you are saying that, at this point, one is just and the other unjust?
> JFL: No. I am saying that they are incompatible. I am not judging. (p. 68)

To most on the left this response would be unacceptable (whether they espoused the cause of the Red Army Fraction or not), as would Lyotard's further description of the Kantian, Hegelian or Christian view of what constitutes injustice as just so many 'motifs', 'almost in the sense of embroidery' (p. 69). Ultra-pluralism of this stamp would be seen to serve the cause of political reaction rather than a left-revolutionary politics, in the sense of presenting no challenge to the status quo.

The End of 'Rational Politics'

Lyotard also takes apart the concept of 'rational' politics, in effect all political theories which conceive of themselves as a 'science' and trade in the business of 'scientific' judgements (the liberal humanist tradition no less than the Marxist):

> For me, rational politics, in the sense of the concept, is over, and I think that is the swerve of this *fin-de-siècle*. We have had an attempt, since the Jacobins, to elaborate and implement a rational politics; this attempt has been pursued throughout the nineteenth and most of the twentieth; it is presently collapsing. And that is a very good thing. (p. 75)

Against 'scientifically judgemental' rational politics, with its tendency towards ' "rational terrorism" in matters of history and political decisions' (p. 74) is ranged, predictably enough, pagan politics. Pagan politics is explicitly linked to the tradition of the classical Sophists,[6] and the Sophists, as Lyotard is quick to point out, always evinced a deep suspicion regarding the notion of rational knowledge:

> they have always indicated that we are dealing with what they called *phantasmata*, that is, representations, and that it is not true that a rational *knowledge* of social and political facts is possible, at least insofar as they imply judgements and decisions. (p. 75)

To his credit, Thébaud is never content to leave things at a pass like this and continues to the end of the proceedings to pose the obvious, and awkward, questions as to how we discriminate between one political position or another, one discourse or another, even managing to win the grudging agreement from Lyotard that,

> it is now a matter of doing a politics of opinions that would give us the capacity of deciding between opinions and of distinguishing between what is just and what is not just; and to have this capacity of deciding, one must effectively have an Idea; but, in contradistinction to what Kant thought, this Idea is not, for us today, an Idea of totality. (p. 88)

The precise nature of this 'Idea' is never very clearly defined, although it seems to gesture towards the 'war on totality' that is called for in *PC*. That merely takes us back, however, into the murky world of self-justifying, and largely self-interested, little narratives. What comes through strongly in Lyotard's postmodernism is how much it functions as a negative theory: it is invariably easier to see what he is against (and why he is against it) than what he is actually for. Thébaud's persistence helps to establish this with commendable clarity in *JG*. The 'Idea' of justice is eventually a regulatory one, although as Samuel Weber points out in his 'Afterword' to *JG*, that seems uncomfortably close to a metanarrative function. Lyotard argues that,

> the Idea of justice resides precisely in keeping prescription in its 'proper' order, just as it does in keeping narration and description in the order that is respectively 'proper' to them. That is, it consists in

maintaining them as different games that cannot have the value of sources of universal obligation. (p. 97)

Weber's rejoinder is that this is to reintroduce the factor of domination by a back-door route:

> By prescribing that no game, especially not that of prescription, should dominate the others, one is doing exactly what it is simultaneously claimed is being avoided: one is dominating the other games in order to protect them from domination . . . Does the referee play? Or does he only judge? (p. 105)

The objection is a perceptive one in that if the Idea were ever put into practice it would have to start dealing in rules, codes of conduct, and, presumably, penalty sanctions against those who did not adhere to the rules or codes of conduct. At that point the 'referee' would take on an aura of authority that placed her or him above the participants in the language games. If on the other hand the Idea remains simply an Idea, an abstract counter in an intellectual *game*, then it can have no political impact in what Lyotard claims in *PC* is a fundamentally agonistic world.

Weber also sees an internal contradiction in Lyotard's position in that incommensurability of the kind argued for in *JG* precludes the agonistics identified as the natural state of affairs of the realm of language games in *PC*:

> as soon as the 'field' of such an agonistics is conceived of as being constituted by absolutely incommensurable, and thus essentially determinable, games, the agonistic aspect is paradoxically restricted by that of the *system* – in other words, by the idea of a finite system of rules, without which it would be impossible to conceive of a game being absolute in its singularity. From that moment, struggle is no longer possible outside of a game, but that game as such is not in struggle, and cannot be. For struggle could only be a form of communication with another game, and that, according to *Just Gaming*, is precisely what should not take place. (p. 104)

The objection is that we can have incommensurability or we can have agonistics, but we cannot have *both*; incommensurability implies the impossibility of agonistics, agonistics demands the absence of incommensurability. One suspects that, for all his love of the figure, that is not the kind of paradox that Lyotard would wish to generate. Nor is agonistics necessarily the positive condition pictured by Lyotard in *PC*; Weber refers us to its Nietzschean form, a darker state which 'always contains an element of domination, a desire to lay hold of the other, to curtail the otherness upon which the agonistics nevertheless depends' (p. 107). Nietzsche addresses us from within a world in which grand narrative holds sway of course (although in his own way he is trying to overcome the condition through his championship of a 'revaluation of all values'[7]), whereas Lyotard is theorizing the postmodern condition beyond the reach of grand narrative. But one might wonder whether the post-metanarrative world remains much more than an ideal that Lyotard provides no practical programme for realizing.

Incommensurability

Incommensurability is certainly emphasized strongly in *JG*'s closing stages, with Lyotard insisting that,

> Not only is there an incommensurability within a game between the position of recipient and that of utterer, for example . . . but, from game to game, for the 'same' position, there is incommensurability: it is not the same thing to be the recipient of a narrative, and to be the recipient of a denotative discourse with a function of truthfulness, or to be the recipient of a command. (p. 94)

One can see the force of Weber's objections at such points: when Lyotard argues for an incommensurability between the 'same' position from game to game, he is echoing the belief of Heraclitus that 'one can never step in the same river twice', and that surely prohibits the development of agonistics. Agonistics assumes some kind of competing interest, but if we can never step in the same river twice it is hard to see how such a state of affairs could ever come about. There is an ambiguity at the close of *JG*, therefore, as to whether incommensurability *is* the case, or whether incommensurability should be *made* the case. If we are to assume the latter, then we are certainly presented with a programme for action (although a strange one to prosecute); if the former, then we should have no problem in the first place. Lyotard contends that, 'It must be understood that if one wants criteria in the discourse of justice one is tolerating de facto the encroachment of the discourse of justice by the discourse of truth' (p. 98), but the persistence of such encroachment would seem to suggest that incommensurability goes largely unperceived by the majority, which makes one wonder whether Lyotard is lapsing back into something like the 'false consciousness' argument; things really are incommensurable, such an argument would go, but because of remorseless cultural conditioning by grand narratives few people are able to recognize that this is so. Again, one suspects this is not quite what Lyotard had in mind.

'Justice' stands revealed as the desire to exercise totalitarian control, whereas the Idea of justice would be the condition where such a totality was given no opportunity to operate. Against Weber's contention that this is to allow totality in by the back door under another guise (through the agency of the 'referee' who enforces compliance on behalf of the Idea of justice), we have Lyotard's claim that every clash of interest will be treated on its own merits: 'when the question of what justice consists in is raised, the answer is: "It remains to be seen in each case"' (p. 99). Leaving aside for the moment the question of how such conflicts could occur if incommensurability really were the case, we might note how close Lyotard's vision of the world operating according to the Idea of justice is to the more idealized version of free market capitalism, where the 'hidden hand' of the market regulates its workings to ensure that self-interest never outstrips the common interest (a comparison laden with irony for such a confirmed anti-capitalist as Lyotard). In a late twentieth-century society few are willing to take quite such a sanguine view of the market's ability to be self-regulating and self-correcting, and one might be similarly inclined to scepticism about the Idea of justice always winning out over the interests of competing language games and their proponents. It would be nice if the desire for totalitarian control were so easily deflected, but one fears it is no more simple to achieve than curbing the excesses of the free market has proved to be throughout the 1980s and 1990s.

It is clear, however, that the thrust of the book is very much against the formation of anything that may aspire towards domination. At the very least incommensurability is to be encouraged (although it is difficult to say what this actually calls for us to do in real terms, and, in truth, it is a rather odd idea), and judgements of all kinds, including judgements of justice, are to be conducted on a case-by-case, rigorously singular basis without reference to any discourse-transcendent criteria. Thébaud's niggling criticisms suggest a fear that justice under such a dispensation will become ever more subject to the workings of personal prejudice, and that remains a considerable worry which Weber's identification of several loose ends in Lyotard's overall conceptual scheme does nothing to dissipate. While we might applaud Lyotard's desire for a domination-free environment, a very real question remains as to whether the Idea of justice he is propounding in *JG* would in actual fact achieve this objective. 'I judge. But if I am asked by what criteria do I judge, I will have no answer to give' does not inspire a great deal of confidence in this respect.

CHAPTER FIVE

'The time has come to philosophize': The Differend

Lyotard clearly regards *The Differend* as one of his most important productions, sometimes even implying, as Geoff Bennington has pointed out, 'that all the work preceding *Le Différend* is more or less radically mistaken, and that the new book cancels and supersedes all the earlier books'.[1] *Diff* is a densely structured work, deeply immersed in philosophical history (in many ways it can be considered Lyotard's most philosophically 'learned' book, with its sustained engagements with Plato, Aristotle, Kant, Wittgenstein, et al.), and it is centrally concerned with the issues of judgement, justice and incommensurability, the very title of the book, as Lyotard points out in his Preface, suggesting 'that a universal rule of judgement between heterogeneous genres is lacking in general'. How one proceeds as a philosopher given that philosophically problematical state of affairs is what the book attempts to discover.

The differend itself goes right to the core of the problem of judgement in a postmodern world:

> As distinguished from a litigation, a differend [*différend*] would be a case of conflict between (at least) two parties, that cannot be equitably resolved for lack of a rule of judgement applicable to both arguments. One side's legitimacy does not imply the other's lack of legitimacy. However, applying a single rule of judgement to both in order to settle

their differend as though it were merely a litigation would wrong (at least) one of them (and both of them if neither side admits this rule) . . . A wrong results from the fact that the rules of the genre of discourse by which one judges are not those of the judged genre or genres of discourse. (p. xi)

The postmodern world is a world of discrete genres of discourse which can no longer be subsumed under any master grand narrative. There is, in other words, no transcendental source of legitimation, therefore no way in which any one genre can come to dominate all the others by claiming closer allegiance to that source of authority. How disputes between genres are to be decided is, however, a problem of some substance in such a world, and one that is left essentially unresolved at the end of *JG*. *Diff* is a sustained meditation on just this issue; indeed, one of the claims made for the work is that whereas *PC* and *JG* made it clear what the concerns of a postmodern philosophy should be, *Diff* actually engages directly with those concerns, that it *does* postmodern philosophy rather than merely *describes* what that activity might be. 'The time has come', Lyotard declares, 'to philosophize' (p. xiii), in order to address the problems of a world weary of theory and its internal battles. In many ways *JG*, with its still largely unconvinced interviewer at the debate's close, reveals the necessity for a project like *Diff* with its apparent 'mission to explain' (although Lyotard cannot resist falling back on the 'message in a bottle' attitude on occasion, as when he remarks that *Diff*'s author 'will never know whether or not the phrases happen to arrive at their destination' (p. xvi)).

Preface: Reading Dossier

Lyotard's 'Preface: Reading Dossier' outlines the project's concerns, methods and field of operations in notably brisk fashion under a series of category headings: Title, Object, Thesis, Question, Problem, Stakes, Context, Pretext, Mode, Genre, Style, Reader, Author and Address. These categories are worth dwelling on for a moment for the light they shed on the project in general (in effect, the conceptual baggage that the author brings to it), even if such a practice does run the risk of enabling certain readers, as Lyotard somewhat contemptuously remarks, 'to "talk about the book" without having read it' (p. xiv).

Object, Thesis and Question establish the centrality of the 'phrase' (or 'sentence' as it might also be translated[2]) in the project to come. The phrase is in some sense a foundational entity, the only object in *Diff*'s discourse 'that is indubitable', or 'immediately presupposed' (p. xi). Nor can one doubt that one phrases, because silence too counts as a phrase (rather in the way that not choosing counts as a form of choice in Sartre's existentialism perhaps[3]). All phrases are subject to rules, or a 'regimen', and there are several such regimens to note ('reasoning, knowing, describing, recounting, questioning, showing, ordering', for example). Phrases link together, and it is the question of *how* they link onto each other that particularly exercises Lyotard, since there is no longer any general rule governing this procedure in a postmodern world. What there is instead is a constant collision of different phrase regimens, a series of differends that occurs because the various phrase regimens are not heterogeneous. This raises the problem of judgement in a stark form: phrases cannot *not* link, 'another phrase cannot not happen', but then neither can differends *not* occur. Conflict cannot be avoided, Lyotard maintains, and it is impossible to remain in a state of indifference. We are back with a vengeance in the world of agonistics rather than the world of discrete discourses pictured in *JG*, where an intrinsic incommensurability seemed, in Weber's reading of it anyway, to preclude the possibility of agonistic conflicts ever occurring. The problem that such conflict and impossibility of indifference sets us is precisely one of judgement: 'to find, if not what can legitimate judgement (the "good" linkage), then at least how to save the honor of thinking' (p. xii). Saving the honour of thinking will be the task reserved for the philosopher.

Philosophy itself is seen to be in a state of differend with regard to two main adversaries, that of economic discourse (capitalism) and academic discourse (the desire for mastery over other, possibly all, discourses). It is Lyotard's goal to construct a 'philosophical politics apart from the politics of "intellectuals" and of politicians', that is, to stake out an area free from the expansionist imperative, a kind of neutral territory where reflection can take place without threat. A politics of this description presumably would also be free from the self-interest that, in Lyotard's view of things, invariably taints the actions of intellectuals and politicians (viz. his reading of the Algerian war of liberation, the *événements*, and the actions in general of all committed Marxists and proponents of grand narratives). A philosophical politics would also enable us to bear witness to the differend in the cultural context of a world where there has been a progressive decline of all metanarratives and universalist discourses, and therefore a foregrounding of the fact of differends. Bearing witness takes on a positive character as the act whereby the right to compete in language games is ensured.

Lyotard situates himself in philosophical history (see Pretext) with particular reference to the work of Kant (*Critique of Judgement*, historical-political texts) and the later Wittgenstein (*Philosophical Investigations*, posthumously published writings), both of whom are considered to gesture towards postmodern philosophy. Lyotard interprets the history of philosophy as an opposition between the modern and the postmodern, that is, an opposition between those who defend universalist discourses and those who undermine them, or at least decline to come to their aid. Thus Kant and Wittgenstein (or at least the part of their oeuvre mentioned above) can be coopted into the postmodern project on the grounds that, 'They draw up the affidavit ascertaining the decline of universalist doctrines (Leibnizian or Russellian metaphysics). They question the terms in which these doctrines thought they could settle differends (reality, subject, community, finality)' (p. xiii). Husserl and Descartes, on the other hand, can be consigned to the camp of the modern for failing to offer a rigorous enough critique of universalist metaphysics. Although both the latter start from a position of doubt regarding truth and knowledge, each manages to resolve it in his own way and to find a foundation for philosophical discourse (the *cogito*, the *epoché*[4]). It is that disposition towards foundationalism which announces that we are in the presence of modernity to Lyotard, who is unambiguously signalling his anti-foundationalist credentials at such points.

Following on from Weber, however, one could query whether an insistence on anti-universalism and anti-foundationalism is not in effect a universalist demand in its own right: in which case Lyotard becomes tripped up by his own critique. One might also speculate as to whether the division of philosophical history into 'moderns' and 'postmoderns' (perhaps the late twentieth-century

version of the 'ancients' versus 'moderns' debate?) would fall foul
of Derrida's critique of binarism. It certainly seems to close off
debate in a way that poststructuralism is wont to regard as authoritarian, with more than a hint of a totalizing vision lying behind
the modern/postmodern division. At least implicitly we have what
amounts to a criterion of judgement here: anti-universalist/
postmodern good, universalist/modern bad. Why we should accept this particular criterion is by no means clear just yet, and
Lyotard has the task of convincing us in the critique to follow.
Disclaimers of the nature that, 'Unlike a theoretician, he does not
presuppose the rules of his own discourse, but only that his discourse too must obey rules', are hardly enough to dispel our
doubts regarding the integrity of the author's own anti-
universalism either, especially when his stated objective is 'to examine cases of differend and to find the rules for the heterogeneous genres of discourse that bring about these cases'. Not for
the first (or last) time postmodernism suggests a desire to have
one's cake and eat it too.

  There are in fact a series of disclaimers to note (and query) in
the Preface, as Lyotard attempts, in what we can now recognize as
entirely characteristic fashion, to manoeuvre himself into a position invulnerable to criticism. The book's mode, we are informed,
is philosophic and reflective, but 'In the sense of poetics', therefore
presumably not to be analysed (or more to the point, perhaps,
judged) in terms of the rules, or regimen, of logical discourse. It is
also described as being in the mode of a metalanguage, but in the
linguist's sense rather than the logician's, so a logically motivated
philosophical critique is deflected (or at least, warned off) yet
again. A 'zero degree style' (p. xiv) is sought for, and if it is not
always attained and a stray note of 'wisdom' unwittingly creeps in
against the author's intentions, the reader is admonished to disregard it. The book itself is disarmingly described as 'discontinuous' in form (an essay rather than a severely logical treatise),
and a mere 'pile of phrases' (pp. xiv, xv). Further, the author does
not know (perhaps he does not really care?) whether his 'pile of
phrases' will ever reach its destination. Taken together, such disclaimers at the very least discourage criticism; indeed their message seems to be that criticism is a misplaced activity in this
context. One is expected instead to 'bear witness' to the project
being undertaken, which is all very convenient for the author. The

'hands off' style of postmodern discourse reasserts itself after the debate format, restricted though it often was in practice, of *JG*.

The tone of the Preface is, as I have indicated, fairly brisk and business-like, although occasionally also prophetic and millenarian – as when we are assured that books will cease to exist in the next century. Books simply take too long to process, Lyotard concludes, and will be replaced eventually by various other means of electronic packaging that save precious time (the postmodern world being an intensely time-conscious one, for reasons that will be explored in more depth in *In*). Lyotard pictures himself as the last of a dying breed, and he sounds distinctly impatient for the coming world of advanced postmodernism where the philosopher's sole concern will be 'the *Is it happening?*' (p. xvi). This commitment to 'writing the event', as Bennington terms it,[5] with its clear echoes of Lyotard in his apocalyptic mode of 1968, is also an uncompromising rejection of everything that grand narrative stands for: order, predictability and the dominance of theory, for example. Addressing phrases to the unknown (the events of an unpredictable and largely unshapeable future) would be anathema to a Marxist theorist, but to Lyotard it is a philosopher's proper occupation. The quasi-Marxist of Barry Smart's reading of later Lyotard is hard to locate at junctures like this.[6]

Idioms and the Differend

The main text of *Diff* consists of a series of numbered paragraphs exploring the condition of phrases and their regimens, interspersed with 'Notices' on the work of a selection of philosophers ranging from Plato and Aristotle through Kant and Hegel to Wittgenstein and Levinas, where Lyotard's arguments are related back to philosophical history. These notices will be considered separately after the main text.

Lyotard is at pains to impress upon us the necessity of recognizing the existence of various phrase regimens, of distinguishing clearly between them, and acknowledging that none can or should legislate outside its own domain. As a philosopher it is his duty, he informs us, to become involved in 'limiting the competence of a given tribunal to a given kind of phrase' (p. 5). A differend is the outcome when those limits are exceeded:

> A case of differend between two parties takes place when the 'regula-
> tion' of the conflict that opposes them is done in the idiom of one of
> the parties while the wrong suffered by the other is not signified in
> that idiom. (p. 9)

As an example of just such a case Lyotard cites the worker–
employer relationship within bourgeois capitalism, where the
worker's labour is treated (and legally recognized) as a commodity
to be bought and sold by the employer on the open market. Within
this idiom there is no other way of describing economic exploitation except as the sale of one's labour power, which puts a gloss of
spurious legality on what the worker perceives in a very different
light. 'In failing to have recourse to this idiom', Lyotard notes, 'the
laborer would not exist within its frame of reference, he or she
would be a slave. In using it, he or she becomes a plaintiff. Does he
or she also cease for that matter to be a victim?' The worker is to
be regarded as the victim of an idiom which has chosen to disregard the rights of other idioms as well as its own idiomatic limits;
but one cannot establish victim status while under the control and
jurisdiction of a dominating idiom, and, as Lyotard quite reasonably observes, it is hard to see what tribunal could pass judgement
on such a matter. The differend, in other words, is simply

> not a matter for litigation; economic and social law can regulate the
> litigation between economic and social partners but not the differend
> between labor-power and capital. By what well-formed phrase and by
> means of what establishment procedure can the worker affirm before
> the labor arbitrator that what one yields to one's boss for so many
> hours per week in exchange for a salary is *not* a commodity? . . . The
> differend is signaled by this inability to prove. (p. 10)

Hence the silence of the victims in the face of domination by
imperialist-minded idioms; hence too, Lyotard's concern with the
setting of limits to tribunal scope and competence.[7] The political
agenda of *Diff* is clear to see, with the silence of the victims of Nazi
concentration camps in the face of demands from revisionist anti-
Semitic historians for conclusive proof of Auschwitz, forming the
sombre backdrop to Lyotard's enquiry into tribunal competence
and the mechanics of phrase regimens.

The differend is the state, therefore, where 'something "asks"
to be put into phrases, and suffers from the wrong of not being

able to be put into phrases right away'. What Lyotard wants to specify is the conditions under which that wrong, which manifests itself as a gut feeling as much as anything else, could be given the opportunity of a voice. To give the differend 'its due' would be 'to institute new addressees, new addressors, new significations, and new referents' for the phrases of the wronged party, with Lyotard insisting that 'Every wrong ought to be able to be put into phrases' (p. 13). A new competence is called for that will ensure this condition can be brought about, and here the philosopher, amongst others (novelists and poets also being cited), finds his or her true vocation in helping to find idioms for suppressed phrases. Now we have something more like a positive programme for philosophical enquiry, as opposed merely to decrying the machinations of grand narrative theorists, and that is to work to establish new idioms where phrases presently silenced by dominating idioms can find expression. This attraction towards the unknown, which by definition cannot exist within the framework of a universalist theory with its assumption of a totalizing vision which shapes all events to its own ends, is what keeps open the gulf between Lyotard and Marxist theorists, who could easily enough concur with his analysis of the worker–employer relationship under bourgeois capitalism, but not his proposed remedy for it. For the Marxist theorist it is a case of the wrong idiom being in control, and all that is required is to substitute the right (that is, dialectical materialist) idiom in its place for justice to be done; for Lyotard, on the other hand, it is a question of challenging the notion of there being a 'right', or naturally superior, idiom at all. Justice in Lyotard's analysis amounts to the assurance that no one idiom will be able to silence the phrases of another. Whereas Marxist philosophers are claiming the right to speak for the silent, postmodern philosophers, by seeking new idioms, are attempting to create the conditions for the silent to speak for themselves. Between the two positions lies a considerable differend.

Postmodern philosophers have a key role to play, therefore, not only in finding new idioms but also in helping to regulate existing ones (seeing that no unjustified linkages are made, prescriptives derived from descriptives, etc.). Linkage is a complex issue, since 'to link is necessary', but 'how to link is contingent' (p. 29). At this point we can have recourse to genres of discourse which establish rules for linkage, but very soon we run up against the problem of incommensurability again, since 'Inside a genre of discourse, the linkings obey rules that determine the stakes and ends. But between one genre and another, no such rules are known, nor a generalized end' (p. 30). It is the problem that always has to be faced in the absence of grand narratives, and it is the area in which the philosopher has to be active. In the first instance we can see the philosopher's task as an educational one, in making us realize that there is no final court of appeal:

> One defers to the 'tribunal of history,' Hegel invokes the 'tribunal of the world.' These can only be symbols, like the last judgment. In what genre of discourse, in what phrase family would the supreme tribunal be able to render its judgment upon the pretensions to validity of all phrases, given that these pretensions differ according to the families and genres to which they are attached? (p. 31)

Having brought us to acknowledge this state of affairs, the philosopher can move on to the higher level objectives of a philosophical politics: seeking out new idioms, guaranteeing the conditions for participation in idioms, helping to promote suitable linkages, witnessing differends, and 'writing the event' in the service of the unknown. Philosophical politics constitutes a space in which we can tackle the injustices and abuses of power associated with a grand narrative culture.

Auschwitz and the Revisionists

One of the most shocking injustices and abuses of power to be generated by that grand narrative culture in the twentieth century has been the system of Nazi concentration camps, with Auschwitz as its most emotive example. Lyotard is much exercised by this phenomenon in *Diff* (as well as elsewhere in his writings), particularly in terms of its treatment by revisionist historians, and he takes the latter to be one of the critical test cases for a philosophical politics.[8] A prime target is Robert Faurisson, for whom, notoriously, the holocaust is a myth:

> I have analyzed thousands of documents. I have tirelessly pursued specialists and historians with my questions. I have tried in vain to

find a single former deportee capable of proving to me that he had really seen, with his own eyes, a gas chamber.[9]

Faurisson's denial of the existence of death camps like Auschwitz is to Lyotard a particularly sinister example of what can happen when genres of discourse are allowed to encroach on each other, and linkages are constructed with ideological ends in view (the besetting sin of 'politics' in the old sense). It is also a classic example of what is wrong with intellectual, as opposed to philosophical, activity. The intellectual is always concerned to prove a case, and, as here, to try to impose conditions of 'proof' so strict that they can be all but impossible for one's opponent to meet. Frustrating one's opponent, turning his or her lack of proof against him or her as proof of one's own thesis, becomes more important to the intellectual than bearing witness to the silencing of victims.

Lyotard is quick to point out just how unrealistic Faurisson's demands are:

> To have 'really seen with his own eyes' a gas chamber would be the condition which gives one the authority to say that it exists and to persuade the unbeliever. Yet it is still necessary to prove that the gas chamber was used to kill at the time it was seen. The only acceptable proof that it was used to kill is that one died from it. But if one is dead, one cannot testify that it is on account of the gas chamber. (p. 3)

What is happening here in Lyotard's view is that verification procedures are being taken as the test of reality, so that 'no verification, no reality' ('no report from inside a gas chamber, no death within a gas chamber') is the criterion being applied by revisionists. The idiom neatly turns silence to account in a clear demonstration of its differend with a philosophical politics, where the objective would be urgently to find some idiom in which the silence could be broken. That is precisely the objective motivating Lyotard in his engagement with Faurisson and his revisionist colleagues. The argument is that reality should not be made dependent on the verification (or the verifier) of it, and, as Lyotard notes, to do so is to run counter to our normal idea of reality:

> we think something is real when it exists, even if there is no one to verify that it exists: for example, we say that the table is real if it is

always there, even if there are no witnesses to the place that it oc-
cupies. (p. 32)

Lyotard might well have inserted a 'Berkeley Notice' at this
point, since this philosopher is probably the most notorious example in philosophical history of where such strict demands for
verification can lead us. Berkeley managed to disprove the existence of material substance, except when it was perceived, so that it
could indeed be argued that when there were no witnesses the
table really did not exist. As far as objects were concerned, their
existence *did* depend on their being perceived, hence Berkeley's
well-known musings about whether 'the tree in the quad' outside
his room existed when he was not looking at it. The way out of the
conundrum for Berkeley was to posit God as a co-perceiver, whose
constant attention to all objects in the universe guaranteed their
continuing existence when Berkeley's perception was not present
(a solution not open to everyone in a post-religious universe); but
he does stand as an instructive warning of the perils of over-
zealous verification procedures, and Lyotard is quite right to object to similar moves on Faurisson's behalf.[10] After all, as Lyotard
points out, 'no one can see one's own death', but no one seriously
doubts the fact that all individuals die. Similarly no one can 'see'
reality, since 'That would be to suppose that reality has a proper
name, and a proper name is not seen' (p. 33). The error Faurisson
has committed is to fail to make the distinction between the phrase
regimens of naming and showing. One can sense Lyotard's anger
at the spectacle of an event of the holocaust's cultural importance
being reduced to an exercise in philosophical gamesmanship.

Lyotard's concern is to avoid solutions along Berkeleyan lines that
require recourse to a transcendental signified (in whatever form it
assumes). His own projected solution drives a wedge between revisionist scepticism, with its demand for personal verification, and
philosophies which take refuge in the transcendental signified option:

> That referent is real which is declared to be the same in these three
> situations: signified, named, shown. Thus, respectively: in an intern-
> ment camp, there was mass extermination by chambers full of Zyklon
> B; that camp is called Auschwitz; here it is. A fourth phrase states that
> the signified referent, the named referent, and the shown referent are
> the same. (pp. 42–3)

What has to be overcome in such cases as Auschwitz is 'the subordination of the question of truth to the doctrine of evidence' (pp. 45–6), a technique that Lyotard finds only too common in the history of philosophy. Auschwitz is far more than a question of evidence, and it requires the historian to be sensitive to the silence surrounding the event, 'to what is not presentable under the rules of knowledge'. The factor of non-presentation is not to be read as proof of there being nothing to present, which is precisely the assumption made by the revisionist school, whose insistence on keeping reality closely tied to verification discloses a more sinister intent on the part of its members, Lyotard claims, and that is to seek to exterminate the memory of Auschwitz along with the fact of the event itself. It is almost as if the revisionists believe that the use of logic can banish the name from the historical record, and Lyotard warns us to be on our guard against such a cunning strategy with its strong appeal to our 'rational' faculty:

> The 'revisionist' historians understand as applicable to this name only the cognitive rules for the establishment of historical reality and for the validation of its sense. If justice consisted solely in respecting these rules, and if history gave rise only to historical inquiry, they could not be accused of a denial of justice. In fact, they administer a justice in conformity with the rules and exert a positively instituted right.

But justice in Lyotard's sense, the guarantee of the right to phrase and to bear witness, is not merely a matter of 'respecting rules'. Lyotard's justice comes into sharp collision with 'Justice' at such points, as it did in the case of the employee–employer relationship under bourgeois capitalism. The philosopher's duty under such circumstances is to respect not the specified rules, but the continuing silence 'which calls upon unknown phrases to link onto the name of Auschwitz' (p. 57); in effect, to keep the name in play as a focal point for the feelings that survive all attempts by interested parties to exterminate even the memory of Auschwitz.

As we have already seen in *JG*, feeling plays a prominent role in Lyotard's philosophical politics. In terms of Auschwitz, feeling is the residue left over from the silence that the revisionists interpret as lack of proof of the event's occurrence. 'The silence imposed on knowledge does not impose the silence of forgetting', Lyotard contends, rather 'it imposes a feeling' (p. 56), and it is this feeling that must be respected by all of us post-Auschwitz: the feeling that impels us to find 'unknown phrases to link onto the name of Auschwitz'. Lyotard's demand that feeling be introduced into the debate echoes not just *JG* but also the turn to the body we identified in *LE*, and it is all part of a concerted challenge running throughout poststructuralist thought to the tradition of rationality that constitutes the paradigm of Western philosophy. Rationality, so this challenge goes, has its limitations (which it generally refuses to acknowledge), and it can be, and all too often is, used to justify some quite barbaric acts (one thinks of Foucault's various historical analyses at this point[11]). Some sort of equation between that tradition and the mentality that could perpetrate (and then later deny) Auschwitz is, provocatively enough, being implied by Lyotard in *Diff*, perhaps along the lines of Auschwitz representing an extreme example of what can happen when differends are allowed to flourish unchecked, and grand narratives are not persistently called to account by a philosophical politics.

Auschwitz is a highly emotive topic, and while one can certainly take issue with the implication that as an event it is bound up with a certain tradition of rational thought, what its use by Lyotard does bring out is just how much is at stake in the development of a philosophical politics. Differends are not mere abstract speculations, but phenomena regularly encountered down at the level of everyday existence (one is even tempted to say right down at *gut* level, given Lyotard's insistence on feeling's role in the process of bearing witness). The argument that Lyotard is above all a political thinker is borne out by the foregrounding of the political here in what I have suggested is his philosophically most 'learned' book. The charge of apoliticism laid at the door of so many poststructuralists and postmodernists is certainly not applicable in Lyotard's case, and in that sense we can note a recurrent concern throughout his career with the political dimension to theory. In fact, foregrounding that dimension can be considered one of the most characteristic traits of Lyotard's analytical method.

Phrases, Genres and Incommensurability

The relationship between phrase regimens and genres of discourse raises the issue of incommensurability in an insistent form.

Lyotard even speculates as to whether incommensurability is a hallmark of the postmodern condition: 'Is this the sense in which we are not modern? Incommensurability, heterogeneity, the differend, the persistence of proper names, the absence of a supreme tribunal?' (p. 135). Phrases present universes, and,

> For every phrase regimen there corresponds a mode of presenting a universe. A genre of discourse inspires a mode of linking phrases together, and these phrases can be from different regimens. The universe presented by a cognitive and the universe presented by an exclamative are heterogeneous. The stakes implied in the tragical genre . . . and the stakes implied in the technical genre . . . are, for their part, incommensurable, and they induce heterogeneous linkings, be they on the basis of the same phrase. (p. 128)

Each regimen, therefore, has its own specific mode of presenting a universe, and no one mode can be translated into another: incommensurability must always occur. The question that Lyotard feels impelled to address at this point is whether teleology applies either *within* or *across* genres of discourse. Acting as devil's advocate, he considers some of the arguments for this possibility:

> You say that a genre of discourse imprints a unique finality onto a multiplicity of heterogeneous phrases by linkings that aim to procure the success proper to the genre. If this is the case, it follows that the heterogeneity of phrase regimens is not of such a kind that it would prohibit their common subordination to a single end. The abyss that separates them would then be, if not filled in, at least covered over or spanned by the teleology of genres of discourse. (p. 129)

He also considers the possibility that all genres of discourse are inspired by the same, and universal, principle of winning or gaining an advantage over other discourses, even if the nature of that victory or gain can vary quite significantly in each case. Nor is incommensurability necessarily immune from this same line of argument; along with the differend and the lack of a supreme tribunal to judge differends, it might merely be part of a new narrative: 'Are "we" not telling, whether bitterly or gladly, the great narrative of the end of great narratives?', Lyotard asks (p. 135). The presence of an 'end', in itself, arguably might be considered enough to keep us within the terms of reference of the modern.

Lyotard is able to circumvent such claims for the persistence of teleology by a close analysis of the relationship between phrases, phrase regimens and genres of discourse. There is no 'first phrase' in a genre; each phrase enters into a sequence of linkages stretching back into the past (Derrida is similarly sceptical of the notion of 'origins'[12]), which 'are ready to take the phrase into account and to inscribe it into the pursuit of certain stakes' (p. 136). But there are many possible ways of reaching these stakes and 'winning'. It is necessary to distinguish, as Lyotard observes that Wittgenstein also does, between the rules of a game and the recommendations as to how to form a strategy to win that game. 'Genres of discourse are strategies', Lyotard asserts, 'of no one' (p. 137). The lack of a human dimension is crucial to his argument. Genres of discourse involve stakes, attainment of any of these stakes counts as success, and success signals conflict along the way; but the conflict is not between human beings but phrases. It is phrases that are always at stake in any differend between genres of discourse, and there can be no 'supreme genre' that settles all such differends:

> the idea that a supreme genre encompassing everything that's at stake could supply a supreme answer to the key-questions of the various genres founders upon Russell's aporia. Either this genre is part of the set of genres, and what is at stake in it but one among others, and therefore its answer is not supreme. Or else, it is not part of the set of genres, and it does not therefore encompass all that is at stake, since it excepts what is at stake itself . . . The principle of the absolute victory of one genre over the others has no sense. (p. 138)

Given the lack of this absolute victory, it also makes no sense to speak of an overall teleology (the same argument can be brought to bear on the issue of authority to disprove the possibility of there being any supreme authority, politically or otherwise). A genre cannot, by definition, act as a transcendental signifier, thus exercising control over all other genres (although it might compete with other genres over phrase linkages). Neither can we speak of teleology in the stricter sense within a genre if the particular mode of winning is not specified in advance; rules alone, so the argument appears to go, do not make a teleology.

It is worth noting that Lyotard does not consider politics to be a genre, rather it is,

> the multiplicity of genres, the diversity of ends, and par excellence the question of linkage . . . it bears witness to the nothingness which opens up with each occurring phrase and on the occasion of which the differend between genres of discourse is born. (pp. 138, 141)

A philosophical politics involves the search for differends and for as yet unknown idioms in which to phrase them. Politics in its more usual sense, the politics of politicians and intellectuals, is, on the other hand, the attempt to ignore differends in the cause of advocating one's own genre to the exclusion of all others (rather in the way that Marxist theorists simply refused to acknowledge the differends of the Algerian situation in the 1950s and 1960s, on the supposition that their genre of discourse was the superior one). The problem with politics as it is usually practised in the West (the characteristic split between left and right in other words), is that narratives which are fundamentally incommensurable (the narrative of the authoritarian state versus the narrative of the liberation of humanity) continue to act as if one eventually could attain superiority over the other. It is this widely held misconception as to what politics really is about that a philosophical politics seeks to correct; bearing witness to differends replaces the drive towards a politics of redemption, whatever part of the political spectrum the latter may be derived from.

Narratives and History

The issue of narrative, and its relation to history, is taken up in more detail in the closing stages of *Diff*, with the Cashinahua yet again featuring as a source of examples as to how narrative can circumvent the legitimation problem and thus evade the clutches of imperialist grand narrative. One of the issues exercising Lyotard is whether any narrative (historical, religious, or national, for instance) can come to take precedence over others in the same genre of discourse. The answer is yes: 'one can be judged stronger than the other if it comes nearer the goal of narratives: to link onto the occurrence as such by signifying it and by referring to it.' An outstanding example of this historically would be the eventual success of the Christian narrative in ancient Rome, which in Lyotard's view succeeded in vanquishing all other narratives of the time 'by introducing the love of occurrence into narratives and narrations of narratives', and in so doing 'designated what is at stake in the genre itself' (p. 159). Christianity, and particularly the concept of Christian love, allowed for linking onto other narratives and genres (indeed it positively encouraged this in its desire to spread the 'good news'), in the process breaking through the constraints of traditional narrative. The Christian narrative's openness to new links enabled it to overtake the weaker, self-contained narratives of the time which simply withered away (one assumes a postmodern politics is designed to have the same effect on narratives such as the Marxist).

Against this positive side of Christianity, however, has to be set the fact that ultimately it is a grand narrative with a transcendental signifier (God), which places strict obligations on the individual believer (with sanctions built in for non-compliance), and as Lyotard notes, 'Obligation cannot engender a universal history'. Love, on the other hand, can, if it is 'supplied with its narrative of authorization', in which case history becomes the 'progress towards the redemption of creatures' (p. 160). Take away the religious authorization, and love survives in a secular form as a politics of redemption (French Revolutionary republicanism or Communism, for example), but that merely raises once again the issue of the differend that obtains between the Idea of freedom and the various narratives of legitimation.

Marxism is seen, at least initially, as an attempt to address a historical differend: the clash between capital and the working class in the nineteenth century. The wrong that is done the working class 'results from the fact that all phrase universes and all their linkages are or can be subordinated to the sole finality of capital . . . and judged accordingly' (p. 171). Marx's narrative project, entirely laudable in the first instance as Lyotard is only too willing to acknowledge, is to discover the idiom in which the working class can voice its opposition to capitalist exploitation. This unusually positive interpretation of Marxism is soon undercut by Lyotard's argument that Marx is a 'prisoner of the logic of result' (p. 172) and its assumption of an ideal, emancipated self (each member of the proletariat) demanding action on its own behalf. From a recognition of the differend we have slid into grand narrative and the politics of redemption. Soon we have the Communist Party imposing its own narrative over the multiplicity of little narratives that go to make up the working class (Lyotard is invariably impatient with attempts to gloss over individual difference and to treat people as totalities), and, in the process, suppressing the very differend that had provided the motivation for the construction of the Marxist narrative in the first place. We have moved from the genre of cognitive phrases (those of the historian, socialist or economist) into the speculative genre: from the physical world to the metaphysical one might say. Marxism constitutes a cautionary tale for Lyotard of what can occur when the incommensurability of genres of discourse is not respected; in effect, once this happens injustice swiftly follows.

'Notices' on the History of Philosophy

The various 'Notices' that break up the text of *Diff* take its arguments more self-consciously into philosophical history, which, as we have already seen, Lyotard conceives of as a conflict between proponents of the modern and the postmodern. Lyotard reads the differend back into the work of several philosophers; Levinas's revealing to us, for example, 'the differend between the ethical phrase (infinity) and the speculative phrase (totality)', and Kant's 'the dispersion of the genres of discourse' (pp. 115, 130).

All too often Lyotard finds the differend being occluded by philosophical sleight of hand or slavish rule-following. Not too many philosophers seem keen to bear witness to its existence. We observe the sophist Protagoras using the paradox of self-reference to win a litigation with one of his pupils, thus wittily, and craftily, preying upon the commonly held belief in a 'supreme genre encompassing everything that's at stake'; Gorgias ignoring the incommensurability between genres of discourse to construct a dialectical argument disproving the existence of being; and Plato espousing a Theory of Forms which in its commitment to absolutism represents an attempt to suppress the appearance of the differend (Socrates' 'simulated' dialogues being designed to that express end). Not surprisingly, Lyotard is highly critical of Plato's attitude to the differend, as well as of the authoritarian overtone of his dialogues, where there is no more than the appearance of agonistics, a mere simulation whose real goal is the absorption of differends and the repression of certain phrases at the expense of others. Platonic dialogue is constructed in such a way as to curtail the very possibility of bearing witness; there is no real dispute being conducted.

Aristotle, on the other hand, is used to back up Lyotard's conception of the occurrence, the unknown event to which phrases are supposed to be addressed. When a phrase occurs, it 'is chained, registered, and forgotten in the occurrence of this phrase, which, in stating the *There is*, binds the occurrence by comparing it with its absence'. A universe is presented, but as we acknowledge the fact of presentation it has already moved on into the unknown, incessantly seeking out new linkages. Anxiety attaches to this state, as Lyotard makes clear in a passage of somewhat purple prose:

> But you wrote: 'For there to be no phrase is impossible' . . . That's just it: the feeling that the impossible is possible. That the necessary is contingent. That linkage must be made, but that there won't be anything upon which to link. The 'and' with nothing to grab onto. Hence, not just the contingency of the how of linking, but the vertigo of the last phrase. Absurd, of course. But the lightning flash takes place – it flashes and bursts out in the nothingness of the night, of clouds, or of the clear blue sky. (p. 75)

Although Hegel's dialectic holds out the promise of such anxiety, with its goal that 'is incessantly attained and accordingly never attained' (p. 96), it is nevertheless ultimately a teleology, if a highly sophisticated one, driven by a specific goal (the same objection can, of course, be laid at Marxism's door, with Marx as the 'prisoner of the logic of result'). Contra-Hegel and Marx, Lyotard is demanding that philosophy be both goal- and result-free:

> The stakes of philosophical discourse are in a rule (or rules) which remains to be sought, and to which the discourse cannot be made to conform before the rule has been found. The links from phrase to phrase are not ruled by a rule but by the quest for a rule. (p. 97)

We are always heading into unknown phrase universes in search of space for the differend to be phrased, and should be doing so without any preconceptions. Close though the Hegelian dialectic is to this condition it is still in some sense prejudging the *Is it happening?* The whole idea of there being a philosophy of history is to Lyotard 'an illusion born from the appearance that signs are exempla or schemata' (p. 171), rather than a series of *Is it happenings?*

One objection that could be made to Lyotard here is that to disregard history as a series of lessons (and they need not be so tightly specified as in either Hegel or Marx's case), is to inhibit the recognition of there being a pattern to abuse of the differend that we can work collectively to overturn. History as a series of *Is it happenings?* is hard to turn to account as a force for social change.

Kant's third *Critique* is taken to reveal the extent of the differend's field of operation. In the *Critique*'s Introduction, Lyotard claims, 'the dispersion of the genres of discourse is not just recognized, it is dramatized to the point that the problem posed is that of finding "passages" (*Uebergänge*) between these heterogeneous genres'. The image this suggests to Lyotard is an archipelago, where 'Each genre of discourse would be like an island' (p. 130). Following up the image, Lyotard suggests that we should consider the faculty of judgement to be something like a body launching expeditions to the archipelago's various islands, in order to present to each island what was found in the others. This information can be used to validate the genre's operations in each case, but there is no totalizing vision lying behind it and the validation is offered on an 'as-if' basis only. No supreme genre is in evidence (the faculty of judgement simply making contacts) and each island remains independent.

The passages are across the differends between each genre, and in that sense Kant can be claimed as a philosopher who both recognizes the differend and avoids the teleology of those later result-oriented dialecticians, Hegel and Marx. To sail around the archipelago is, in Lyotard's scheme of things, to seek new phrase universes.

The Politics of Phrasing

The differend, Lyotard concludes, 'summons humans to situate themselves in unknown phrase universes, even if they don't have the feeling that something has to be phrased. (For this is a necessity and not an obligation)'. This summons is to be understood in a positive sense, its continual, necessary, occurrence keeping at bay economic genres, with their desire to exercise hegemony over individuals and communities. The sheer heterogeneity of phrase universes, regimens and genres of discourse, is our best defence against imperialist-minded genres and grand narratives. Lyotard remains uncompromisingly anti-teleological in his thinking, insisting that there is no pattern throughout history (except those false patterns imposed by interested parties motivated by a politics of redemption), merely 'occurrences', that is, events whose character cannot be judged or predicted in advance (the final challenge of *Diff*, in fact, is 'Are you prejudging the *Is it happening?*'). Occurrences cannot be turned into a narrative, not even the narrative of a political programme: all one can do is bear witness to them. The politics of phrasing turns out to be a non-, or even an anti-politics in our traditional understanding of political activity.

For all his anti-capitalist sentiments, it is at points like this that Lyotard provides the basis for the critique which aligns postmodernism with neoconservative politics.[13] The New Right is just as keen at breaking down institutional structures and setting the individual free to pursue his or her little narrative amongst a multiplicity of other little narratives similarly engaged, just as suspicious of the motives of big government with regard to little narratives as Lyotard implies postmodernists should be; and even if they do differ in their attitude to capitalism, what else is the latter but a series of events, *Is it happenings?* (unexpected market booms, downturns, new phrase universes, etc.). Lyotard even suggests that capitalism has something of the sublime in it. The same criticism can be made of Lyotardean philosophical politics (and often is) as of unfettered free-market capitalism: that for every individual it empowers to realize his or her own little narrative, it leaves countless others at risk from unexpected, and frequently personally catastrophic, occurrences. The rather bleak picture we might take away from *Diff*'s closing stages is of an isolated and bewildered individual lost in a world of seemingly random occurrences. When Lyotard argues that 'there is not "language" and "Being," but occurrences' (p. 181) it hardly suggests a world in which the human dimension counts for very much.

We can also query whether creating new idioms for phrasing is enough in itself to bring about the end of social wrongs. Ensuring that every wrong is 'put into phrases' is not the same thing as ensuring that those wrongs will be ended. What the latter depends on is a wholesale change of attitude throughout society which it is hard to envisage at the moment (the voluntary relinquishment of grand narrative power, for example). An obvious question to come to mind is what happens if not everyone cooperates in this radical shift of paradigm? Even if they do, one can easily imagine a situation in which a babble (and a constantly growing babble at that) of little narratives cancelled each other out, in which wrongs might well be phrased but little attention was paid to them. It is a moot point who would benefit from such a state of affairs, even if it did have the desired effect of precipitating the end of grand narrative as we know it.

In the final analysis, it can be objected that what Lyotard himself is offering in *Diff* is, in its call for humanity's emancipation from grand narrative and the attendant abuse of phrase regimens and genres of discourse, nothing less than yet another politics of redemption (his own devil's advocacy is more persuasive than dissuasive on this score). Leaving aside the irony of this result, one could say that, as is so often the case with such phenomena, not all parts of the programme for redemption are equally desirable, or for that matter practicable.

CHAPTER SIX | 'Svelteness' and 'paganism'

Postmodernism's suspicion of authority in almost all its forms calls for a different mode of individual conduct, one far less hidebound by conventional rules and regulations and more open to new experience. We have already seen how the rejection of grand narrative leads to a concomitant support for open-ended, non-imperialist little narratives where individuals can engage in agonistically structured games of move and countermove with each other, and we can now consider just what kind of behaviour this assumes it is appropriate to adopt at individual level. Two key concepts put forward by Lyotard in this respect are 'svelteness' and 'paganism', both of which involve a flexibility of response on the part of individuals that is essentially foreign to the world of grand narrative, where rules and regulations dictate prescribed patterns of public behaviour.

'A Svelte Appendix to the Postmodern Question'[1]

Svelteness features prominently in an essay entitled 'A Svelte Appendix to the Postmodern Question' (1982), included in the collection *Tombeau de l'intellectuel et autres papiers* (1984).

Although short, this is a striking piece (for all that Lyotard presents it in throwaway fashion as merely 'A few remarks, devoid of theoretical pretensions, and in no particular order' (*PW*, p. 25), but then, perhaps that is a characteristically postmodern mode?): a densely packed set of observations which touch on a wide range of postmodern preoccupations on the way to presenting the concept of svelteness – 'wakefulness, a Zen and an Italian term' (p. 28) – as a politically highly desirable trait to cultivate.

The thrust of the piece is to establish capitalism as the greatest problem of today's society, one that even overshadows that posed by the bane of most late twentieth-century leftist intellectuals, the contemporary state. For all his post- and even anti-Marxist sentiments Lyotard still has not lost his suspicion of capitalism, and, as we shall see in Chapter 10 when we go on to look at *The Inhuman*, it is a suspicion that remains a critical aspect of his repertoire. Capitalism is treated in 'Svelte Appendix' as another name for modernity, and further, in its seemingly insatiable appetite for domination of the world around it, as the very essence of romanticism (even partaking of 'something of the sublime', as Lyotard remarks elsewhere[2]). Its goal is to conquer the cosmos (in effect all sources of energy) in the name of the will. In this respect it is the enemy of both the contemporary state (with its obsessive love of order) and of social tradition (with its equally obsessive love of rules); capitalism cuts across these as the explosive force of desire:

> capitalism derives its force from the Idea of infinity. It can appear in human experience as the desire for money, the desire for power, or the desire for novelty. And all this can seem very ugly, very disquieting. But these desires are the anthropological translation of something that is ontologically the 'instantiation' of infinity of the will. (p. 26)

Neither is capitalism the preserve of any particular social class (Lyotard taking yet another dig at Marxist verities), it cuts across class just as sharply as it does across the state and social tradition: 'There is no class that incarcerates and monopolizes the infinity of the will', it is argued, not even the 'owners or the managers of capital'. Capitalism comes to seem an exemplification of that 'insinuation of will into reason', leading to the 'drive of reason to go beyond experience', which Kant for one was so aware of in his philosophy. And even Kant can be claimed for the cause of the postmodern in some sense, since he saw it as philosophy's duty 'to create differends' (p. 26). (Presumably Lyotard has the 'antinomies of pure reason' in mind at this point, although it could be countered that Kant's objective was not so much to *create* such antinomies, which he took to be evidence of philosophy's failings, as to find a way to *resolve* them. If, on the other hand, Lyotard is referring to Kant's division of reality into 'noumenal' and 'phenomenal' realms, then it is a moot point whether these can be regarded as differends in Lyotard's sense of the term.)

The 'invasion' of this capitalist 'will' into the domain of language, one of the characteristics of the transition from modern to postmodern society, has some potentially very far-reaching consequences for the way we live. Lyotard notes the tendency for language to be turned into information, a commodity that can be bought and sold on the open market, and speculates that, 'Under the guise of an extension of markets and a new industrial strategy, the coming century is that of the investment of the desire for infinity, according to the criterion of optimum performance, in matters of language' (p. 27). Given that language is also 'the whole social bond', there is the very real possibility that the relentless expansion of capitalism eventually will undermine society. Lyotard will go on to explore the threat posed by advanced capitalism ('development' as he dubs it, linking it up to the revolution in contemporary techno-science) in more detail in *The Inhuman*, a rather sombre work which paints a fairly depressing picture of the likely coming world order (see Chapter 10), but he does offer us some ray of hope here in 'Svelte Appendix' as to how resistance can be mounted to capitalism's restless dynamic. 'Our role as thinkers', it is claimed, 'is to deepen what language there is, to critique the shallow notion of information, to reveal an irremediable opacity within language itself' (p. 27); that is, to point up the incommensurability of the various phrase regimens that go to make up language (the point that had been made so forcefully in *Diff*). Postmoderns – and the term is broad enough to encompass Freud, Duchamp, Bohr, Gertrude Stein, Rabelais and Sterne – can resist the fragmentation of the social bond by stressing and generating paradox, thus refusing to let language be commodified into saleable units of information. Recent French philosophy – Derrida, Foucault, Serres, Levinas, Deleuze, for example – amounts to just such a project of resistance, in Lyotard's view, by its repeated emphasis on the pervasiveness of incommensurability in discourse (taken collectively, the philosophers above might even be regarded as the effect of the figure within discourse).

It is here that svelteness comes on the scene, with its characteristics of 'flexibility, speed, metamorphic capacity'; 'Svelteness, wakefulness, a Zen and an Italian term' (in Italian literally 'slenderness', as in its use in fashion terminology) which is above all 'a quality of language, because it takes very little to create the new (Einstein in Zurich)' (p. 28). 'The infinity of the will', Lyotard insists, has to come to terms with svelteness, with its creative, inventive, and perhaps most important of all in this context, unpredictable qualities at individual level, and this can have a politically beneficial effect for society: 'much less "working," much more learning, knowing, inventing, circulating. Justice in politics lies in pushing in that direction' (pp. 28–9). The cultivation of svelteness plus incommensurability is the basis of a project to counter the inhuman drive towards the 'informationization' of discourse that marks out contemporary capitalism. Lyotard's point seems to be that no matter how inhumanly mechanistic capitalism becomes, it cannot altogether eradicate the possibility of resistance being mounted by individuals through the medium of language; language, handled with svelteness (which has a certain guerrilla-like quality to it), has the capacity to prevent capitalism's total victory. It is a theme, as I have said, that Lyotard will go on to explore in greater detail, and perhaps with less sense of optimism about the future, in *In*.

'*Lessons in Paganism*'[3]

Paganism, 'the denomination of a situation in which one judges without criteria' (*JG*, p. 16), plays an increasingly important role in Lyotard's later thought, almost amounting to a political programme in its own right. Judgement without criteria takes place, significantly enough, in matters of aesthetics, ethics and politics as well as of truth. Neither postmodernism nor paganism is to be understood in a periodizing sense. In each case we are dealing with a cyclical phenomenon that flourishes in the absence or decline of grand narrative. Thus we can learn from the paganism of the past, that of Aristotle and the sophists, for example, how to operate in a contemporary

situation of general 'incredulity towards metanarratives'; a situation
where, as Lyotard puts it in 'Lessons in Paganism',

> for the first time in fifty years, most of your country's intellectuals are
> not prepared to tell and justify even an updated version of the Marxist
> narrative because they take the view that it has had profoundly unjust
> effects wherever it has been fully implemented. (*LR*, p. 123)

When even intellectuals, notorious for their defence of grand narratives in the teeth of evidence to the contrary, turn against Marxism it is time to ask what the next step should be politically.

'Lessons in Paganism', with its sprightly dialogue form, suggests what kind of political programme is appropriate to paganism
in the later twentieth century:

> So, alternate between harassing the State and harassing capital. Attack
> them by attacking their pragmatics. And if it is at all possible to do so,
> use one to attack the other . . . use laws and institutions against the
> abuses committed by entrepreneurs, organize tenants' associations,
> shopfloor struggles, ecological campaigns . . . And use the opposite
> argument, and the right to be an entrepreneur, when it is a matter of
> checkmating some dangerous state monopoly: set up pirate radio sta-
> tions, invent unorthodox teaching methods (as at dear old Vincennes),
> try to unionize soldiers or prostitutes . . . (p. 152)

In its flexibility, speed and metamorphic capacity, this is effectively svelteness by another name, and it retains much of the
optimism of a 1960s-style activism. As a programme it is highly
pragmatic (the lack of any Marxist grand narrative baggage is very
apparent in the suggestion that, depending on the circumstances,
one either fights entrepreneurs or becomes one), and not very
likely to win general acceptance on the left, especially when the
speaker freely admits to a gradualist approach, replying to the
challenge of his interlocutor that 'You won't win any lasting victo-
ries' with a casual 'I don't expect to. We have to take our time'
(p. 152). Pagan resistance is not undertaken in the name of totality,
therefore, but in that of the multitude of little narratives that make
up human history. History, we are told,

> consists of a swarm of narratives, narratives that are passed on, made
> up, listened to and acted out; the people does not exist as a subject; it

is a mass of thousands of little stories that are at once futile and serious, that are sometimes attracted together to form bigger stories, and which sometimes disintegrate into drifting elements, but which usually hold together well enough to form what we call the culture of a civil society. (p. 134)

All this is a long way away from the totalizing imperative of Marxism, and a graphic illustration of how poststructuralist thinkers are now willing to challenge the Marxist reading of history. History is no longer to be viewed as an inexorable progress towards a predetermined goal which theory can clearly specify the nature of, but rather as a random and chaotic, even libidinal, process of shifting allegiances, temporary alliances and drifting elements, in which no one story ever has the right to dominate.

The narrative aspect is emphasized, with the pro-paganism speaker remarking that,

> don't forget that when I draw your attention to a few minor political matters and issues in contemporary history, I am merely telling you a story, unfolding a little story of my own. As a preliminary lesson, I would suggest that, rather than asking if that story is more or less true than any other, you should simply note that it exists, that it is the product of an almost invincible power to tell stories that we all share to a greater or lesser extent . . . and that it leaves you all the time in the world to tell a very different story about the same historical and political points should you choose to do so. (pp. 125–6)

What is to be resisted is the grand narrative tendency (as usual Marxism provides the outstanding example) to absorb all these little narratives and alternative readings into a single, totalizing narrative that systematically downgrades individual experience. The lesson of 1968, where a host of new narrators, narratees and stories suddenly came onto the scene without any official permission, is that this process is well under way; and the proliferation of such stories, it is insisted, can only be for the public good:

> We should be struggling to include metanarratives, theories and doctrines, and especially political doctrines, in narratives. The intelligentsia's function should not be to tell the truth and save the world, but to will the power to play out, listen to and tell stories. (p. 153)

Another area where suppressed narratives are beginning to be told without any official permission being sought, is the women's movement, and this too can be seen to further the cause of paganism, given that 'the feminine principle . . . closely resembles my pagan principle';[4] as Lyotard remarks in 'One of the Things at Stake in Women's Struggles':

> women are discovering something that could cause the greatest re-
> volution in the West, something that (masculine) domination has
> never ceased to stifle: there is no signifier; or else, the class above all
> classes is just one among many; or again, we Westerners must rework
> our space-time and all our logic on the basis of non-centralism, non-
> finality, non-truth.[5]

The women's movement is a movement of resistance against the totalizing imperative, here identified as a specifically Western discourse, or 'phallocracy', and we might see this as yet another instance of the work of the figure that discourse – whatever it may think – can never capture.

Ultimately, what paganism directs us to do is to undermine the authority of grand narrative by whatever means come to hand, even if it is a case of becoming an entrepreneur to achieve that objective. To be pagan (or svelte) is to be an irritant to the powers-that-be, a constant reminder in one's person of where totality breaks down. The political message we are invited to take away from the 'Lessons' is 'Destroy narrative monopolies' (p. 153) in the name of the infinite proliferation of little narratives, and it is a political message that is as hostile to the left as it is to the right. Lyotard's outlook remains revolutionary, but a considerable gap now separates it from what the organized left would find acceptable as political activism.

CHAPTER SEVEN | *The sublime*

The sublime plays an increasingly significant role in Lyotard's later thought, and we find in particular repeated engagements with the Kantian notion of the sublime. Lyotard sees the Kantian sublime as being closely bound up with the notion of modernity, the latter being a phenomenon characterized by 'a shattering of belief' and the 'discovery of the "lack of reality" of reality' – themes only too familiar to us from modern art and literature, where the experience of alienation figures so prominently (what else does a Kafka character feel, for example, but the ' "lack of reality" of reality'?). Nietzschean nihilism is one expression of this 'lack of reality', the Kantian sublime another – and the aesthetic of the sublime is argued by Lyotard to be the major impetus behind modernism in the arts.

Kant's philosophy assumes that human subjects possess both a faculty of conception and a faculty of presentation: knowledge results when the objects presented by sense conform to our conception of them, when, as Lyotard puts it, 'if, first, the statement is intelligible, and second, if "cases" can be derived from the experience which "corresponds" to it' (*PC*, p. 77). When it comes to the arts and the concept of taste (defined as 'the principle of a universal consensus'),

> Taste . . . testifies that between the capacity to conceive and the capacity to present an object corresponding to the concept, an

undetermined agreement, without rules, giving rise to a judgment which Kant calls reflective, may be experienced as pleasure. (pp. 77–8)

The reflective judgement (in Lyotardean terms of reference, a judgement without criteria) links the object of beauty (the work of art) and the concept of beauty, but there are cases where this link cannot be made, cases where pain is the experience rather than pleasure and that Kant subsumes under the heading of 'the sublime'. The sublime involves cases where 'the imagination fails to present an object which might, if only in principle, come to match a concept'. Cited as examples of such failures to make the required match are our ideas of totality and infinity; while we can conceive these (the totality of the world, the infinitely powerful, etc.) we can never make them visible – or to be more precise, any attempt on our part to present such ideas can only strike us as 'painfully inadequate' (p. 78). These are ideas which preclude presentation, and which can tell us nothing about reality. Hence the importance of the sublime for modern artists, concerned as they are to communicate modernity's 'shattering of belief' and 'discovery of the "lack of reality" of reality'. Such an art, given its subject matter, is, of course, unlikely to be a source of pleasure (unless one wants to speak of 'the pleasure of a displeasure' (*Diff*, p. 165)), and the attraction of the sublime becomes evident.

Lessons on the Analytic of the Sublime

Lyotard's most sustained engagement with the Kantian sublime comes in *Lessons on the Analytic of the Sublime*, modestly enough presented as 'a file of notes in preparation for the oral explication of the Analytic of the Sublime (Kant's *Critique of Judgment* §§23–9)'[1] in *explication de texte* mode, but in reality having the more ambitious design of establishing the sublime as a model for reflexive thinking in a world under the sign of the differend. We are to be offered a new reading of Kant's third *Critique* in *LAS*, which challenges the widely held view that it achieves its stated objective of repairing the divisions left in philosophy by the first two *Critiques* (*Pure Reason* and *Practical Reason* respectively). As Lyotard points out, the *Critique of Judgment* sets itself the task of unifying philosophy, of being, the sought-after 'bridge' between the theoretical and the practical, spanning the gulf previously created between the knowledge of objects according to the conditions of possible experience and the realization of freedom under the unconditional of moral law. (p. 1)

Lyotard vigorously contests the viability of such a project. The aesthetic, he is to argue, cannot provide such a bridge and ultimately only makes us more keenly aware of the incommensurabilities between different phrase regimens (we can recall his earlier conception, in *Diff*, of the faculty of judgement as a body launching expeditions over the passages between genres). In other words, Kant's attempt at unification merely reveals the pervasive influence of the differend throughout our discourses. Kant is to be read through the differend, with the emphasis falling on any incompatibilities or aporias in his thought.

It will come as no surprise, therefore, that what Lyotard finds in Kant's treatment of the sublime, the condition where we are confronted by the unpresentable, is, precisely, a tacit recognition of the existence of the differend and an invitation to bear witness to it. The sublime is where Kant's unification project irretrievably loses its way, where the faculties of conception and presentation just cannot be brought into alignment:

The relation of thinking to the object breaks down. In sublime feeling, nature no longer 'speaks' to thought through the 'coded writing' of its forms . . . Above and beyond the formal qualities that induced the quality of taste, thinking grasped by the sublime feeling is faced, 'in' nature, with quantities capable of suggesting a magnitude or a force that exceeds its power of presentation. (p. 52)

To unify philosophy would be to reconcile nature and freedom, but since the sublime amounts to 'an aesthetic without nature' (p. 54) it can hardly contribute to such a project. What the sublime demonstrates is the impossibility of that project ('A meteor dropped into the work' (p. 159) in Lyotard's words), and, as is the case with the event, we can do no more than bear witness to this state of affairs, which is described by Lyotard in highly dramatic language recalling that used in introducing libidinal economy:

Sublime violence is like lightning. It short-circuits thinking with itself. Nature, or what is left of it, quantity, serves only to provide the bad contact that creates the spark. The teleological machine explodes. The 'leading' that nature with its vital lead was supposed to provide for thinking in a movement toward its final illumination cannot take place. The beautiful contributed to the Enlightenment . . . But the sublime is a sudden blazing, and without future. Thus it is that it acquired a future and addresses us still, we who hardly hope in the Kantian sense. (pp. 54–5)

What the sublime signals is the limits of Enlightenment, and it is this aspect of it that Lyotard wants to emphasize for the postmodern world. From within the heart of the Enlightenment project we seem to have the admission that a totalizing philosophy can never be constructed (totality itself being unpresentable), which of course 'addresses us still' in a culture where grand narratives, with their boundless faith in their ability to represent totality, are being systematically and successfully challenged by thinkers such as Lyotard. The sublime offers a more accurate picture of the world we experience, Lyotard is claiming, than that put forward in the name of Enlightenment, where reason is argued to be in control. Confronted by the sublime, 'Reflection thus touches on the absolute of its conditions, which is none other than the impossibility for it to pursue them "further"; the absolute of presentation, the absolute of speculation, the absolute of morality' (p. 56).

The experience of reaching limits and unpresentable absolutes, in effect of experiencing the differend, is not unexpectedly the source of pain and anguish to the individual. Although the beautiful and the sublime both provide 'delight' according to Kant, the effect of this delight is markedly different. In the case of the beautiful, delight 'is felt "directly" as a "furtherance of life"' (p. 67), with the sublime, however, it

arises 'indirectly' as a feeling of two conflicting moments: the 'vital forces' experience a momentary check, *Hemmung*, an inhibition; they are held back, repressed. When they are released, they 'discharge' – this is the *Ergieflung* – all the more powerfully in the following moment . . . Because of this transitory anguish, the sublime emotion is not like play. In it the imagination is seriously occupied. Contrary to taste, the sublime feeling is an emotion, a *Rührung*, that alternates between an affective 'no' and 'yes'. (p. 68)

Sublime delight is a dislocating phenomenon, therefore, which keeps us uncomfortably aware of the unbridgeable gap between the faculties of conception and presentation, and seems to point to a basic incommensurability within our experience that neither reason nor understanding is capable of resolving. Whereas the aesthetic of the beautiful would seem to provide evidence of there being a bridge between the realms of the theoretical and the practical, of a totalizing philosophy in action in other words, the aesthetic of the sublime consistently seems to announce the impossibility of such totalization ever being accomplished, and to keep bringing us sharply up against reality's lack of reality. The sublime disrupts our cosy world-picture much as the differend invariably does – small wonder then that Lyotard wants to emphasize it so forcefully.

We have seen the importance attached to feeling in Lyotard's philosophy, particularly as regards the act of judgement, and feeling plays a critical role too in the sublime: 'the absolute is not conceived of as an Idea but only felt' (p. 73), it is noted. Absolute greatness, as a case in point, cannot be compared to other greatnesses, it can only be felt: 'is "this" felt to be great, or more or less great? Answer: "this" is felt to be great, absolutely' (p. 79). Kant himself opens the door for feeling when he comments that:

> If, however, we call anything not alone great but without qualification, absolutely, and in every respect (beyond all comparison) great, that is to say, sublime, we soon perceive that for this it is not permissible to seek an appropriate standard outside itself, but merely in itself. It is greatness comparable to itself alone. (quoted, p. 79)

From this line of thought, Lyotard feels justified in pushing the case for the primacy of feeling in reflective judgement, suggesting of absolute greatness, for example, that 'this is judged absolutely great because the thought that judges this feels itself to be great absolutely', and that it has an 'absolute affinity with a finality in itself that it discovers on the occasion of this feeling' (p. 81).

After *JG* we can see where this is leading: to judgement without criteria, based on feeling; that is, to paganism and the guerrilla campaign against grand narrative and its totalizing ways (and paganism involves not just feeling but instinct too[2]). In fact Lyotard goes on to argue that, 'The true name of sublime greatness is magnitude. Magnitude is a subjective evaluation reserved for the faculty of reflective judgment' (p. 82). The sublime provides the conditions for the development of a reflexive thinking based on a recognition of the differend, hence its attraction for Lyotard and postmodern thought.

Lyotard locates a differend right at the centre of sublime feeling, a differend that is the consequence of,

> the encounter of the two 'absolutes' equally 'present' to thought, the absolute whole when it conceives, the absolutely measured when it presents. 'Meeting' conveys very little; it is more of a confrontation, for, in accordance with its destination, which is to be whole, the absolute of concepts demands to be presented . . . This conflict is not an ordinary dispute, which a third instance could grasp and put an end to, but a 'differend'. (pp. 123–4)

The identified differend resists all attempts at its resolution, being reducible, for example, neither to moral feeling nor to the operations of a dialectic. We are left instead with the inescapable and irresolvable '*double bind* in which the imagination is caught and kept prisoner in sublime feeling: to present the unpresentable' (p. 141). Neither can that differend be universally communicated in the way that it is claimed taste, 'the principle of universal consensus', can; sublime feeling being 'neither moral universality nor aesthetic universalization, but . . . rather, the destruction of one by the other in the violence of their differend. This differend cannot demand, even subjectively, to be communicated to all thought' (p. 239). What we can say that the differend at the heart of the sublime *does* demand, is that we bear witness to the impossibility of any bridge spanning the realms of the theoretical and the practical. Kant's unification project, Lyotard concludes, is irremediably undermined, its aporias and incommensurabilities only too clearly visible after the impact of the 'meteor' that is the Analytic of the Sublime.

The Sublime and Modern Art

As we pointed out above, modern art is defined by Lyotard as that art concerned with presenting the unpresentable, 'that there is something which can be conceived and which can neither be seen nor made visible: this is what is at stake in modern painting' (*PC*, p. 78). We shall go on to consider Lyotard's views on art in more detail in the next chapter, but it is worth lingering for a moment here on what he says on the subject in terms of the sublime in 'Answering the Question: What is Postmodernism?'.

Kant's suggestion that the commandment 'Thou shalt not make graven images' is 'the most sublime passage in the Bible in that it forbids all presentation of the Absolute', provides Lyotard with the basis for an 'aesthetic of sublime paintings'. Sublime painting, he argues, would, like any painting, have to present something, but would be required to do so in a negative fashion, non-figuratively or non-representationally. An example cited is K. S. Malevitch's white squares, which 'enable us to see only by making it impossible to see' (p. 78). Enabling us to see by making it impossible to see, and pleasing by causing pain, are effectively the axioms of avant-garde painting, Lyotard maintains, and the sublime can be considered their source: 'They remain inexplicable without the incommensurability of reality to the concept which is implied in the Kantian philosophy of the sublime.' Painting like Malevitch's therefore bears witness to the differend located at the core of modernity as a social project, and that act of bearing witness is seen to be crucial to the avant-garde art of the twentieth century; thus, 'the avant-gardes are perpetually flushing out artifices of presentation which make it possible to subordinate thought to the gaze and to turn it away from the unpresentable' (p. 79).

Modern aesthetics is essentially an aesthetic of the sublime as far as Lyotard is concerned, but he has some criticisms to make of it nevertheless, mainly that it still evinces a certain nostalgia for the 'real' reality that has been lost and the belief that has been shattered – in effect, for the world in which the reflective judgement operated unproblematically. 'It allows the unpresentable to be put forward only as missing contents', and therefore does not quite succeed in communicating, 'the real sublime sentiment, which is an intrinsic combination of pleasure and pain: the pleasure that reason should exceed all presentation, the pain that imagination or sensibility should not be equal to the concept' (p. 81). For that 'real sublime sentiment' nowadays we have to turn to postmodern art and aesthetics.

The Sublime, the Event, and the Differend

It is fairly obvious what the ' "drama" that goes by the name of the sublime' (*LAS*, p. 98) offers to a thinker of Lyotard's stamp. The sublime is a disruptive force (lightning-like, blazing, violent), the experience of which is extremely disorienting and unsettling to the individual, in a manner strikingly similar to the impact of the event, the figure, and the differend. The individual's complacency, product of an Enlightenment-derived world-view which privileges the power of reason, is disturbed in each case, his or her illusion of being in control is shattered, and he or she is forced to acknowledge the necessity of bearing witness to a process over which he or she can never hope to exert any meaningful domination. What the aesthetic of the sublime discloses is the ultimate futility of modernity's project of totalization (the sublime, like the event, being 'without future'), and that is a disclosure to be accepted gratefully by such an anti-totalizing thinker as Lyotard unfailingly declares himself to be. Read through the differend, the sublime does indeed become a model for reflexive thinking in a postmodern age.

CHAPTER EIGHT | Art and artists

Becoming an artist was, as he tells us in the early pages of *Peregrinations*, one of Lyotard's earliest ambitions, and if he never achieved it (we shall see why in Chapter 10), he has maintained a strong interest in art over the course of his career, producing books, essays and contributions to exhibition catalogues on the work of several artists – even organizing exhibitions, such as *Les Immatériaux* at the Pompidou Centre in Paris in 1985.[1] As far as Lyotard is concerned this is no mere sideline to the main business of being a philosopher and cultural critic, but a significant part of his overall project. The emphasis laid on the act of seeing and visual figures in *Discours, figure*, where the figural is seen to be an element perpetually disruptive of rational discourse, indicates how important the visual is to Lyotard's line of thought, and painting under such a dispensation becomes a prime site for philosophical enquiry ('We thought we knew how to see; works of art teach us that we were blind' (*LR*, p. 224).) As David Carroll has observed,

> Probably no philosopher since Merleau-Ponty has been as concerned with the problem of the relation and/or non-relation of painting and critical discourse as has Lyotard, with the way art offers critical perspectives on discourse in general.[2]

We have already seen how Lyotard identifies relations between the Kantian sublime and modern art, arguing that the aesthetic of the sublime underpins such art and its concern to communicate the 'shattering of belief' and ' "lack of reality" of reality' so characteristic of modernity. The aesthetic of the sublime enables artists to bear witness to the differend at modernity's centre, and thus corresponds very closely to the project of a philosophical politics. It is not possible in a study of this length to do any more than just dip into Lyotard's writings on particular artists, and that is what we shall do in order to gain something of a flavour of this material.

Duchamp's Trans/Formers

The work of Marcel Duchamp has exercised a strong fascination on Lyotard, as his book *Duchamp's Trans/Formers* suggests. *DT* is a collection of essays on Duchamp's work, with specific reference to 'The Bride stripped bare by her Bachelors, even (The Large Glass)' and 'Given: 1. The Waterfall, 2. The Illuminating Gas', drawn from various sources such as exhibition catalogues and colloquia on Duchamp's work. What these works in particular convey to Lyotard is a strong awareness of the event and the figure. 'The Large Glass', for example, is neither figurative nor non-figurative, rather 'It figures the unfigurable', in this case 'a figure that could not be intuited – at least that of a woman having four dimensions'.[3] Duchamp constitutes a case study for Lyotard of the relation/non-relation of painting and critical discourse, therefore it is worth dwelling for a while on *DT*'s essays.

Not surprisingly for someone who is so suspicious of capitalism and the ultra-rationalism of contemporary techno-scientific development, one of the main things Lyotard finds to praise in Duchamp's work is its 'pointlessness' (p. 69). Lyotard also speaks approvingly of how Duchamp's 'machinery' is designed to call into question the notion of a 'totalizing and unifying machine' (p. 49), whether in the domain of technology, language or politics. Given Lyotard's consistent opposition to the project of totalization in Western culture, it is not hard to see why he would be drawn to this aspect of Duchamp's art, with its clear suggestion of resistance, in both the svelte and pagan senses, to the imperatives of grand narrative. Despite the fact that there are some quite technical descriptions of Duchamp's machinery – the mathematics and geometry involved, for example – *DT* is not concerned to offer an 'explanation' of the artist's productions. No matter what you say about these productions, Lyotard claims in the opening essay 'Incongruences', there is ultimately 'something uncommentable' about them that defeats traditional critique; as a critic, therefore,

> You'd have to think of a counter-ruse: in what you say about Duchamp, the aim would be not to try to understand and to show what you've understood, but rather the opposite, to try not to understand and to show that you haven't understood. (p. 12)

What you *can* do with works like 'The Bride stripped bare' and 'Given', however, is to draw attention to their refusal to further the cause of grand narrative, with its remorseless drive to assign meaning to artefacts in terms of its overall conceptual scheme – to see even art as part of a larger order. Lyotard's refusal to offer standard commentary, detailing what Duchamp's works 'mean' in the context of recent cultural history ('No, not a commentary on incomprehensibility in general or in particular, the seven hundred and twenty-eighth modern text on modernity as the experience of Nothing' (p. 12)) constitutes a similar refusal to play the grand narrative game. Instead we are to observe Lyotard 'searching among the little notes and improvisations of Duchamp: materials, tools and weapons for a politics of incommensurables' (p. 18).

A large part of Duchamp's appeal lies in his hatred of repeating himself and constant search for new effects. For Lyotard he is a 'transformer' whose art demonstrates that,

> There are only transformations, redistributions of energy. The world is a multiplicity of apparatuses that transform units of energy into one another. Duchamp the transformer does not want to repeat the same effects. That is why he must be many of these apparatuses. He wants to win first prize every time, in all the competitions, for new patents. (pp. 36–7)

Works like 'The Large Glass', with their complex mechanical structure, have uncontrolled effects, which turn them into an unfolding series of events challenging the viewer, whose preconceptions about art are continually displaced (not least by the requirement to 'think' what the work cannot present, such as 'a woman having four dimensions'). The viewer is invited to bear witness to the event as it happens, rather than to have a predictable aesthetic experience which reinforces the grand narrative vision of art and its place in the community. In that respect Duchamp's art does not engage in the circulation of meaning or information that is the hallmark of an advanced capitalist society.

Not even the artist can be said to have control over his productions: 'Duchamp's machines', Lyotard claims, 'are not enslaved-assertive but spontaneous-affirmative', and 'know no consequence' (p. 69). Their sheer pointlessness refers us back to energies that transcend meaning (hence the admonition 'to try not to understand and to show that you haven't understood'); to something like libidinal economy perhaps, which can be felt but never explained as such. One cannot judge Duchamp's machine art in terms of conventional aesthetic schemes, therefore, and rather like sophistic reasoning, where 'the terror of the True or the False has no place' (p. 48), one is forced to judge artefacts like 'The Large Glass' by their effects alone – which brings us into the orbit of paganism. In the best of pagan traditions, Duchamp provides no solace for the guardians of grand narrative: certainly neither 'The Large Glass' nor 'Given' will support any project of totalization, remaining unpredictable and inexhaustible from one viewing-event to the next, one 'now' to the next (as Lyotard notes elsewhere, 'Anyone who looks at the Glass is waiting for Godot . . . One never finishes recounting *The Large Glass*' (*LR*, p. 241)). An art like this can be drawn on by a philosophical politics to offer critical perspectives on discourse in general, since as Lyotard goes on to insist, 'Now makes a hinge between not yet and no longer. That goes without saying for any event, erotic, artistic, political. And does not give place to mysticism' (*DT*, p. 199). Duchamp is clearly on the side of the event, the differend, the figural, the svelte, and the pagan.

Valerio Adami

Duchamp's is not the only way of bearing witness to the event, and several other painters are singled out for praise by Lyotard in this respect. Cézanne, for example, is considered to be particularly attentive to the event and the differend, and succeeds in rendering events as ' "directly" as possible without the mediation or protection of a "pre-text" ' (*Per*, p. 18) in his great sequence of Mont Sainte Victoire paintings; Barnett Baruch Newman's paintings contrive 'to be the occurrence, the moment which has arrived' (*In*, p. 79), in contrast to Duchamp's where we are always on the 'hinge between not yet and no longer'; Valerio Adami, by an 'anamnesis [or 'not forgetting'] of the visible', preserves the singularity of vision without allowing it to be absorbed into some larger grand narrative scheme. Cézanne and Newman will be discussed in more detail in Chapter 10 in connection with *Peregrinations* and *The Inhuman*, but Adami can be considered briefly here.

'Anamnesis of the Visible, or Candour'[4] deals with several Adami works such as *La Tavolá*, *Medea/Beidermeier Zimmer*, *Incantesimo del lago*, and *Omphallos* (the striking image on *LR*'s cover). For Lyotard, Adami's art is marked by a sense of withdrawal, 'As though he were trying to clear the visible . . . rushing towards a candour of vision, towards an other vision' (*LR*, p. 220). The effect of this withdrawal is to pare down the artist's visual language – Adami 'stripping himself of our collective imagery', as Lyotard puts it – which characteristically leaves very few figures (often only one) in the frame. It is an uncluttered art seeking 'the point that exists before there are any knots. The landscape where the knots of history will be tied, where history will build to a climax. A primal landscape' (p. 223); in other words, the point before the intrusion of grand narrative into little – perhaps before the corruption of vision by discourse. Vision and discourse stand opposed, and even if philosophy tells us that vision can deceive, and that science holds out the promise of correcting such deceptions,

> Yet it is still incorrigible, as it is corrected in an order which is not its own, within a system of ideas, whereas its order, the immanence of views is, or so we may assume, disavowed, unauthorized as appearance. Even so, sight still makes the setting sun look bigger. The *logos* may well criticize the delight of seeing; it cannot do away with it. (pp. 232–3)

Between sight and the *logos* lies a differend, and Adami's 'anamnesis of the visible' bears witness to that differend and the singularity, the here-and-now quality, of visible events. Lyotard closes the essay with a plea, on the painter's behalf, for that

differend to be respected: 'Please, I beg you, don't turn my anamnesis into an ideology, a false truth and a false rule for life.' Art is
neither an ideology nor an activity for its own sake, rather an act of
bearing witness: 'No, there's no *for*, because there is no finality,
and no fulfilment. Merely the prodigious power of presentations'
(p. 239). What art provides us with is a means to combat the
totalizing imperatives of the grand narrative tradition.

'*Acinema*'

An interesting insight into what Lyotard expects from, and values
in, the arts in general and painting in particular, can be gleaned
from an essay he wrote on the art of cinema. 'Acinema'[5] makes
clear Lyotard's commitment to experimentalism in the arts (something he repeatedly defends over the course of his career, and has
often been criticized for), and constitutes an attack on mainstream
cinema: in fact, more or less all cinema with pretensions to 'realism'. The crux of the argument is that cinema is in the main a
highly ordered art form, concerned above all with communicating
a sense of unity:

> And the order of the whole has its sole object in the functioning of the
> cinema: that there be order in the movements, that the movements be
> made in order, that they make order. Writing with movements –
> cinematography – is thus conceived and practised as an incessant
> organizing of movements following the rules of representation for
> spatial localization, those of narration for the instantiation of language,
> and those of the form 'film music' for the soundtrack. The so-called
> impression of reality is a real oppression of orders. (*LR*, p. 170)

The anti-authoritarian in Lyotard balks at such an excess of control, which is interpreted as a denial of libidinal economy
('Acinema' dates from 1973 and Lyotard's 'libidinal' phase) as
some kind of mirror image of capitalist economy with its closed
system of exchange.

One might say that what cinema does is to preclude the unpredictable and the unknown, and thus to prevent bearing of witness
to the event. Whereas an art like Duchamp's proudly proclaims its
'pointlessness', everything in cinema is designed to have a 'point'
in terms of the final product: the art of directing in particular (and

here Lyotard is very critical) is precisely the art of selecting what is necessary in order to achieve an overall sense of unity to the film. 'Film direction', therefore, 'is not an artistic activity . . . film direction acts always as a factor of *libidinal normalization*' (p. 175). Direction is for Lyotard essentially a political activity, one more way by which grand narrative's project of totalization is prosecuted.

Lyotard calls for an 'acinema' to challenge the totalitarian ethos of the mainstream variety, and suggests various ways by which it could achieve this aim: by introducing extremes of movement (stasis, disorder, etc.), or by means of abstraction, for example. In the latter case painting might be seen as providing a source of inspiration (Pollock and Rothko are specifically mentioned in this context). What is clear to Lyotard is that the stranglehold of realism needs to be broken, as does the aesthetics of unity.

Various objections can be made to Lyotard's view of the cinema; for one thing the insistence on the politically subversive power of abstraction seems curiously old-fashioned in the late twentieth century (more modernist than postmodernist one is tempted to say), and film theorists would be quick to point out that mainstream cinema is capable of being politically far more subversive than Lyotard is willing to allow. The reduction of cinema to, essentially, movement is certainly contentious as well; not all theorists would be prepared to see it in such exclusively visual terms nowadays (something of the privileging of the visual found in *DF* lingers on here in 'Acinema'). What is clear after considering Lyotard's views on cinema, however, is that he does expect creative artists to exhibit an attitude of suspicion towards notions of unity and totality. If they can do so they can be claimed for the project of a philosophical politics, and their work valued accordingly; if not, then they are consciously or unconsciously serving the cause of grand narrative. Either way, art certainly has a political dimension to Lyotard, and his concern with the political is as evident in this area of activity as it is elsewhere.

CHAPTER NINE | Intellectuals and intellectualism

A key concern of Lyotard throughout his career has been the social role of the intellectual, and he has expressed some considerable reservations about the work of intellectuals in general as well as of his own in particular. We have noted frequent instances of his readiness to criticize, often in the severest possible terms, the nature and terms of reference of intellectual activity, and to question the integrity of those engaged in it. Intellectuals repeatedly turn out to be the villains of the piece in Lyotard's socio-political analyses; figures who put themselves uncritically in the service of grand narrative (being more interested in proving a case than in whether a case is worth proving), and who refuse to bear witness to the differends that philosophers, their mirror image in this reading, are constantly striving to find new phrase universes for.

This is a very French debate, and it is fair to say that intellectuals as a class have in modern times enjoyed a higher profile in France than in most other European countries. Sartre provides an outstanding example of how an intellectual figure can come to take on the status of cultural icon in France, and although it is perhaps overstating the case to speak of existentialism's 'popularity', there is no denying that in the years following the Second World War Sartre's philosophical activities were the subject of considerable media interest.[1] The depth of this interest can be gauged by the fact that his notorious rift with Albert Camus, another outstanding example of the French intellectual class, over Camus's book of political philosophy *The Rebel* (savagely reviewed by an associate of Sartre in his journal *Les Temps Modernes*), made front-page news in France in 1952. Foucault, Derrida, Baudrillard and Lyotard can all be seen as latter-day examples of this class, which, in one form or another, has traditionally been fostered by the state authorities to a degree almost unheard of in most of the rest of Europe.

It is against this background of state institutionalization of intellectual activity that Lyotard's pronouncements on the intellectual class need to be seen – and also, one might conjecture, against a background of youthful Marxist militancy in which intellectual activity was only too likely to be viewed with a certain amount of suspicion (as an elitist activity in comparison to the work of the proletariat or party activists, for example); arguably Lyotard retains something of this anti-intellectualism even after he becomes classifiable as a lapsed Marxist.

The Tomb of the Intellectual

The issue of authority figures very prominently in all this. Intellectuals are accorded a certain degree of authority (perhaps more so in France than elsewhere) and authority, as we are now aware, is one of Lyotard's great obsessions. A deep vein of anti-authoritarianism runs throughout his work, from the Algerian writings of the 1950s to late projects like *In*, and postmodernism is nothing if not an anti-authoritarian project. A brief look through some selections from *The Tomb of the Intellectual*[2] reveals just how jaundiced a view Lyotard has of intellectual 'authority'.

In the keynote essay 'The Tomb of the Intellectual', Lyotard responds in typically iconoclastic fashion to the socialist government's appeal to intellectuals (by whom it felt deserted since its electoral victory) to lead the debate on what French socio-economic reform requires of the nation's citizens, arguing that what the government spokesperson, Max Gallo, is really looking for is technical experts rather than intellectuals. Technical experts are concerned to optimize 'performance', in a 'cost-benefit' sense, whereas intellectuals, are more like thinkers who situate themselves in the position of man, humanity, the nation, the people, the proletariat, the creature, or some such entity. That is to say, they are thinkers who identify themselves with a subject endowed with a universal value so as to describe and analyze a situation or a condition from this point of view and to prescribe what ought to be done in order for this subject to realize itself, or at least in order for its realization to progress . . . The responsibility of 'intellectuals' is inseparable from the (shared) idea of a universal subject. (p. 3)

There is in fact a clear distinction in the responsibilities of the two groups, although Lyotard is no more enamoured of intellectuals than he is of 'cost-benefit' analysts. Putting it in the bluntest possible terms, he argues that 'There ought no longer to be "intellectuals"'; history has passed them by in the sense that the idea of a universal human subject is now largely discredited, as is the notion of any universalizing thought: 'it is precisely this totalizing unity, this universality, that thought has lacked since at least the middle of the twentieth century' (p. 6). There is a clear implication that the collapse of the grand narrative ethos has destroyed the foundation of most intellectual activity.

The conclusion to Lyotard's intervention in the looked-for debate would seem to be that intellectuals could not do what the government wants, and that what they actually can do is of no great public use anyway. It is a fairly comprehensive demolition job on the intellectual class, and it is typical of Lyotard that the only groups who come out of this intervention with any great credit to their name are artists, writers and philosophers, whose responsibility lies, not to cost-benefit analysis or some dubious concept of universality, but to their work, and this work is concerned to challenge 'the accepted criteria of judgement in painting, literature, and so forth' (p. 4) rather than to trade on questionable notions of authority for personal advantage. Artists, writers and philosophers have turned their back on the universal in favour of responding to the event and the differend, and thus provide some sort of model as to the kind of figure governments really *ought* to be looking for in a postmodern world:

the decline, perhaps the ruin, of the universal idea can free thought and life from totalizing obsessions. The multiplicity of responsibilities, and their independence (their incompatibility), oblige and will oblige those who take on those responsibilities, small or great, to be flexible, tolerant, and svelte. (p. 7)

When we come to svelteness we have come a long way from authority or the idea that any one individual can meaningfully speak for another for any significant length of time. The svelte thinker keeps phrase linkages open, and as Lyotard notes in 'Wittgenstein "After"':

> One can love a thought. One is not for all that a specialist in this thought, nor capable of explaining it to others. One does not make of it a profession or a vocation. It is 'only' a feeling. A feeling is like a phrase waiting to be formulated. One feels that one is thinking (even if only a little) 'after' this thought. One must, one will have to, link onto it. One tries to find a way. This 'after' is not yet fixed. What is certain is that this thought will be taken into account, and one will be accountable to it. (p. 19)

To keep phrase linkages open is to acknowledge that one can neither own a thought nor use it to ground one's authority over others.

In the final analysis intellectual authority is little better than a confidence trick for Lyotard, and he is scathing of those who perpetrate it for their own self-interested ends. Commenting on the apparent global triumph of capitalism in *The Differend*, Lyotard points out that, 'The intelligentsia is not sparing with its support, its advice, its participation in the new power', but that, 'I believe that the activities of thought have another vocation: that of bearing witness to differends' (p. 10). Once again we are given a clear signal that there is in Lyotard's eyes something basically dishonest about the nature of intellectual activity: an indefensible complicity with the powers that suppress little narratives.

'A Podium without a Podium'

Yet another attack on intellectuals and their pretensions towards authority can be found in 'A Podium without a Podium: Television according to J.-F. Lyotard',[3] the text of a television programme prepared by Lyotard for the series 'Tribune Libre' in 1978. In what the programme producers must have realized afterwards was effectively a hostage to fortune, Lyotard was asked to appear as an 'intellectual'. Not surprisingly, given his low opinion of such beings, he chose to to use his appearance as an opportunity both to criticize intellectuals as a class and to distance himself from that class – Lyotard being a philosopher rather than an intellectual. Thus he can argue that,

> If philosophers agree to help their fellow citizens in authority in matters where there isn't any, to legitimate this authority, then they cease to ponder in the sense in which I spoke of thinking, and they thereby cease to be philosophers. They become what one calls intellectuals, that is, persons who legitimate a claimed competence . . . their own, but persons who above all legitimate the very idea that there ought to be competence in everything. (p. 95)

Competence, like performance, belongs to the world of techno-science, a world inimical to svelteness, differends and events, all the things that philosophers have a responsibility towards – even if not many of them have remained true to their vocation, as Lyotard somewhat despairingly concedes:

> For a long time, in the West, philosophers have been exposed to the temptation of the role of the intellectual, they have been tempted to turn themselves into the representatives of an authority. And there are not many, since Plato, over the past twenty-five hundred years, who have not succumbed to this temptation. It seems to me that Lyotard would like to belong to this minority; that's what he told me to tell you. (p. 95)

Elsewhere, reflecting on traditional philosophy, Lyotard accuses the philosopher of too often being 'a secret accomplice of the phallocrat', and philosophy of being 'the West's madness' which 'never ceases to underwrite its quests for knowledge and politics in the name of Truth and the Good'.[4] The majority of philosophers are seen to be deeply implicated in the project of totalization that Lyotard so abhors.

Proper philosophy, as opposed to mere intellectualism with all its connotations of dilettantism, is therefore something of an act of cultural resistance. The pressure is to conform to the prevailing political regime (what the socialist government's appeal to 'intellectuals' really amounts to, in Lyotard's opinion), indeed, to help to bolster that regime's power and authority. Being a real philosopher, rather than a mere accomplice to phallocracy, is having the courage to stay outside the political mainstream, and to resist its remorseless drive towards order, competence and optimum performance. Aware as he is of the basic disorder of philosophical thought, Lyotard 'thus refuses to appear before your eyes and ears as an authority, as he is asked to do' (*PW*, p. 94). Unlike intellectuals he will decline to provide a public 'service'.

Lyotard employs various distanciation effects throughout the programme to emphasize the lack of pretension to authority in his own person. Initially he is heard but not seen; then he is heard and seen but with the sound out of synchronization with his lips, except for a brief section in the middle when sound and image *are* synchronized. He also refers to himself in the third person throughout ('when he is put in the position of being an authority, as is the case for Lyotard at this moment, he wonders about the authority he is asked to have' (p. 93)). Tiresome though such tricky devices are, they do go some way to undermining the authority of the medium, with Lyotard being concerned to combat the fact that,

> The presence on the screen of the least little philosopher, of the least little handyman, of the least little employee, of the least little variety show artist, devoid of authority as he may be, contributes and even suffices to give them an authority for a few moments . . . (p. 94)

Whether he achieves it or not, the objective is to hold the whole procedure of the construction of authority up to ridicule. Lyotard is simply refusing to play the intellectual game as his society understands it, choosing instead to belong to the awkward minority of philosophical history.

Authority remains the heart of the problem that philosophers have to confront; 'the big question' being, 'the need to believe in an authority, authority's need to be believed, its need to believe in itself' (p. 94). But this is a political rather than a philosophical issue, Lyotard maintains, and one that it is every true philosopher's duty to problematize as much as possible – as Lyotard is clearly striving his very best to do in 'A Podium without a Podium'. The main criticism that emerges of intellectuals in such studies, is that they have failed to see what is really at stake in social existence: philosophers, on the other hand, must continually bear witness to this, no matter what degree of unpopularity the practice may bring them.

| CHAPTER TEN | The peregrinations of a philosopher: Peregrinations and The Inhuman |

The Wellek Library Lectures in Critical Theory at the University of California, Irvine, in 1986, provided Lyotard with the opportunity to define his position as a theorist and to reflect on his career. In their published form as *Peregrinations: Law, Form, Event* (which also includes 'A Memorial of Marxism' discussed earlier) these lectures constitute a fascinating insight into Lyotard's perception of his own development as a philosopher, 'my peregrination' (p. 8) as he refers to it, as well as of his mature perspective on the nature of philosophical thinking itself. The fluidity that characterizes Lyotard's later thought is well captured by the lecture/chapter titles, 'Clouds', 'Touches', 'Gaps', with their implication that the world of thought is shifting and tentative rather than concrete and totalizing: a world where short-term little narratives rather than long-term grand narratives flourish. 'Thoughts are clouds', we are told, whose 'periphery . . . is as immeasurable as the fractal lines of Benoit Mandelbrot' (p. 5). The idea, so deeply engrained in the grand narrative tradition, that we can gain mastery over thought and direct it to specific ends, is, therefore, simply delusive, as is the still commonly held notion that we can plot our own destinies. The uncompromisingly anti-totalizing attitude signals to us the extent of Lyotard's estrangement from the ideals of the Enlightenment project (technological progress, individual liberation, etc.) – ideals that had underpinned the Marxism he once espoused. This is, after all, a thinker who can conclude the account of his 'peregrinations' with the sentiment that, 'It seems to me that the only consensus we ought to be worrying about is one that would encourage this heterogeneity or "dissensus"' (p. 44). Totality is to be firmly, and unconditionally, rejected.

Per is, therefore, yet another argument for the virtues of an agonistic lifestyle, where everything is to be geared towards coping with the singularity of each event on its own terms. It is another one of our common delusions, Lyotard declares, 'to give meaning to an event or imagine a meaning for an event by anticipating what that event will be in reference to a pre-text' (p. 27), whereas what we should be doing is bearing witness to the differend and devising tactics to deal with the consequences of the 'Is it happening?' as it unfolds. *Per* is a revisionist view of Lyotard's own philosophical development, and by implication the history of philosophy, from that post-Enlightenment perspective, such that it is revealed to be a series of peregrinations rather than a triumphal progress towards a specific goal (the resolution of the class struggle, the emancipation of humanity, or any of the various liberationist or redemptionist narratives on offer in the modern world). The choice of the word 'peregrinations' is itself suggestive, putting one in mind of somewhat haphazard rather than goal-directed motion.

'Clouds': Thought and Philosophy

Lyotard is at pains to stress the accidental quality of his choice of profession. He becomes a philosopher only after progressively discarding his earliest ambitions to become either a monk, an artist, a historian or a writer. Attempts at creative fiction, including a novel in the *Nouveau Roman* style, meet with little encouragement; then apparently without any conscious planning Lyotard finds himself in the situation of husband and father, and thus under the pressing necessity of earning a living; finally, he is discouraged from taking up history because of his poor memory. 'Thus I became a professor of philosophy at a lycée in Constantine, the capital of the French department of East Algeria' (*Per*, pp. 1–2): already Lyotard's life is turning into a series of responses to unpredictable 'Is it happenings?'. The fact that he is later to be chosen spokesperson on Algeria for *Socialisme ou barbarie* on the basis of his local 'knowledge', merely reinforces the notion that individual existence owes considerably more to chance than it does to conscious planning. Viewed from such a perspective life is not a neat narrative with a beginning, a middle and an end (and it is in the nature of the modern, Lyotard claims, to insist on such beginnings, middles and ends), but an altogether more random process which, rather like clouds, has no clearly delineated boundaries or pathways. 'Even the story I am in the process of narrating', Lyotard points out, 'reveals that any narrative whatsoever begins in the middle of things and that its so-called "end" is an arbitrary cut in the infinite sequence of data' (p. 2). To think otherwise, to imagine that one can programme one's life, or, more grandly, the course of history itself, is to fall into the delusion of grand narrative.

Lyotard identifies the world of the monk, the painter and the historian with the law, forms and events respectively, but not in any discrete, one-to-one correspondence way; ethics, aesthetics and politics overlap in his work to the extent that they can hardly be detached from each other. Theory becomes an amorphous entity under such circumstances, something fluid and constantly changing that resists the idea of fixed 'positions'; in fact, Lyotard warns us that 'if I am unable to take a position this is due not to a bent toward confusion – at least I hope not – but to the lightness of thoughts'. Such lightness proceeds from the nature of thought:

> Thoughts are not the fruits of the earth. They are not registered by areas, except out of human commodity. Thoughts are clouds. The periphery of thoughts is as immeasurable as the fractal lines of Benoit Mandelbrot. Thoughts are pushed and pulled at variable speeds . . . Thoughts never stop changing their location one with the other. When you feel like you have penetrated far into their intimacy in analyzing either their so-called structure or genealogy or even post-structure, it is actually too late or too soon. (p. 5)

Clearly, if this *is* the nature of thought then all attempts to gain mastery over it, whether in the manner of Lévi-Strauss, Foucault, or even Derrida, are futile. It is in the nature of the beast to resist containment (Wittgenstein's language games are held to function in a similarly uncircumscribable way). From *DF* onward Lyotard keeps identifying entities, or forces, that resist containment in this way, and clouds can be seen to stand in a line that stretches back through the sublime to the figure and libidinal economy. A characteristic Lyotardean image arises of an amorphous force forever eluding the systematizing impulse, with paganism and svelteness constituting socio-political analogues for that elusiveness.

Forget mastery or containment, therefore, at best all we can find are islands of determinism within a larger chaotic structure that will never conform to any teleology we may try to impose on it. It is part of human arrogance to believe that total systems of knowledge can ever be constructed, and in a striking image Lyotard suggests that 'Time is what blows a cloud away after we believed it was correctly known and compels thinking to start again on a new inquiry, which includes the anamnesis of former elucidations' (p. 7). No theory can claim dominion over time, which will ceaselessly present it with the unknown (yet another echo of Heraclitus' dictum that 'you can never step in the same river twice'). Claiming such dominion over time is, of course, precisely what a grand narrative like Marxism does, assuming that the dialectic can be interpreted in the same way indefinitely into the future, yielding the same kind of results that it does in today's world. Lyotard will go on to explore this aspect of time more fully in *The Inhuman*.

Philosophy under such a dispensation as this is hardly the activity of traditional repute, being neither an arbiter of disputes nor a generator of hard-edged, unequivocal, criteria of judgement for general use by other disciplines. All that is left the aspirant philosopher is 'the endless pursuit of the task of discussing clouds' (p. 7), and creative artists such as Sterne, Diderot and Proust are as good guides to how this pursuit should be conducted as any philosopher or scientist (Rorty is later to make a somewhat similar point in *Contingency, Irony, Solidarity*[1]). Neither are we to regard our contributions to the pursuit in question as in any way original ('thoughts are not our own', Lyotard insists (p. 6)), or as constituting anything approximating to a beginning or ending to a narrative: 'I suggest that each thinking consists in a re-thinking and that there is nothing the presentation of which could be said to be the "premiere." Every emergence of something reiterates something else, every occurrence is a recurrence' (pp. 8–9).

The philosopher's task is not system-building, therefore, but *phrasing*, and inasmuch as we can speak of there being any obligation we are laid under in the field of philosophy it is to continue the process of phrasing as best we can: 'There is a necessity for a phrase to be linked with the event as a happening.' To be a philosopher is to be forever aware of that necessity to contribute to the phrase series, and also to have an awareness of how powerless that contribution is to dictate the future course of the thought-cloud. Lyotard's philosopher is a conspicuously humble creature, only too conscious of his or her limitations, of the fact that, no matter what phrase he or she has just added to the chain, linkage between phrases always remains open. Philosophy is the discipline that perpetually bears witness to the fact that no phrase ever possesses the power to close a narrative.

Philosophy is also the discipline that encourages the development of a svelte attitude towards events. Lyotard speaks of a 'probity' with respect to clouds, which takes the form of,

> an ability to be responsive to slight changes affecting both the shape of the clouds you are trying to explore and the path by which you approach them . . . Probity is being accessible to the singular request coming from each of the different aspects. It is a sensitivity to singular cases. (p. 8)

There is a certain law to events, and what that law prescribes is 'a something, a "I don't know what"' (p. 10). The 'I don't know what' may take the form of either action or inaction, but what it does prescribe is that we cultivate a svelte responsiveness to change, and respect the 'lightness' of thought without reference to any pre-text. For all the distance that he has traversed intellectually from his *Socialisme ou barbarie* days, there is a common currency between views such as these and Lyotard's ultimate judgement of what was required of, but sadly not delivered by, Marxism in the Algerian situation in the 1950s and 1960s. There the theory's practitioners (the PCF, etc.) signally failed to exhibit any sensitivity to the singular case with which they were confronted; in other words, they were not open to the reception of a 'I don't know what' which challenged their totalizing vision: Marxism simply could not allow for exceptions to its political rule. It is noticeable that the farther we go in Lyotard's career the greater the degree of suspicion we find him expressing as regards that totalizing imperative and all those who espouse it.

Refusing to heed the call made by the 'I don't know what' is one of the defining characteristics of the grand narrative mode, and Lyotard goes so far as to argue that,

> every writer or thinker carries in him or herself as a particular temptation the weakness or the possibility of ignoring that he or she is committed to a 'I don't know what.' Thus, he or she may trace its path among clouds of thoughts as if not only the tracing but the commitment were not due to an appeal. (p. 12)

With their commitment to defending theses rather than taking risks, intellectuals are presumably a prime example of yielding to just such a temptation, hence Lyotard's contempt for them as a class. To be open to the 'I don't know what', that is, to be a philosopher rather than an intellectual, is to be continually exposed to risk, since the summons put out by clouds of thought 'is not under our control, and we are not entirely determined by it . . . The content of the law being basically unexplicit' (p. 12). Philosophers (of Lyotard's 'minority' kind anyway) bear witness to the openness of the future, whereas intellectuals, to their eternal discredit, go on pretending that their grand narrative theory has explicit pre-knowledge of this, thus laying an unmerited claim on our attention.

Given the inexplicit nature of the law's summons we are entirely justified in relying on our feelings as a guide to how to respond, which Lyotard acknowledges was the procedure he adopted in the writing of *LE*. Twelve years on he now views the book as a testament to 'the dizziness that can take hold of thinking when it becomes aware of how groundless all the criteria are that are used to respond to the requirements coming from the law'. In this reading *LE* becomes something like a rite of passage from the world of metanarrative to that of the postmodern with its inexplicit, but nevertheless demanding, law. Not knowing what this demand is, Lyotard falls back on feeling – gut feeling we might say, given the book's somewhat hysterical tone ('the flesh and blood of words' in Lyotard's own description). *LE* breaks with the tradition of commentary and explanation to become an outburst of feeling in the face of the 'I don't know what' that replaces a faith in Marxism, an attempt at 'inscribing the passage of intensities directly in the prose itself without any mediation at all'. If arguably an 'evil book, the book of evilness that everyone writing and thinking is tempted to do' (p. 13), it is none the less 'an honorable sinful offering', whose 'shamelessness, immodesty, and provocation' (p. 14) constitute a gut reaction to the insistent demands of the 'I don't know what' that most writers and thinkers cannot, or will not, face. The work's 'intensities of affects' may, Lyotard freely concedes, be interpreted as a licence to indulge in 'lawful permissiveness, including violence and terror' (p. 15) (and that is exactly how many commentators have chosen to interpret the postmodern project, as a theoretical free-for-all which might be used to sanction almost anything[2]). But that is the risk we must take if we are to respond without reference to any pre-text to the summons of the law – and it is a risk well worth running. Whatever else *LE* may be, it is not a work founded on the metanarrative delusion that one can exert control over the course of events: postmodern ethics are far less comfortable than that.

'Touches': Art and Politics

'Touches' deals with the *Socialisme ou barbarie* phase of Lyotard's career, and illustrates graphically the way that ethics, aesthetics and politics overlap in his thinking. The depth of his commitment to the group's cause, where, for a period of several years,

> I gave up all writing except notes and studies on political topics that were published either in our review or in a mimeographed paper we gave out to workers early in the morning at the gates of factories or on the occasion of demonstrations,

suggests, as he admits, an attitude of almost 'monastic obedience' (p. 17) on his part. At this point ethics and politics fuse, although that is not necessarily what is wanted in a world of endlessly changing, forming and re-forming, 'clouds'. From a postmodernist viewpoint there is a certain rigidity in the way that Lyotard responds to the call of the period's events. We might note in passing, however, that the single-mindedness Lyotard brings to his *Socialisme ou barbarie* activities is still there in later career in the intensity of his devotion to the differend and the 'I don't know what' – in a sense Lyotard never does lose his monastic bent.

Part of the problem with politics is that it is so concerned to change things rather than to pay attention to the differend and the 'I don't know what'. Art, on the other hand, can be very attentive to these phenomena, as the case of Cézanne would suggest. The series of paintings the artist undertook of the Montagne Sainte Victoire reveals a talent for capturing events in something like a philosophical manner, that is,

> as 'directly' as possible without the mediation or protection of a 'pretext' . . . Cézanne remains motionless while his sight endlessly scans the Montagne Sainte Victoire, waiting for the emergence of what he called 'small sensations,' which are the pure occurrences of unexpected colors . . . This is a singular way of exploring this cloud of thought whose proper name is the Montagne Sainte Victoire. Its singularity lies in how irrelevant for painting pictures are such values as meaning, consistency, likelihood, recognition, identification – one's only concern is to glance at the birth of colors, like the dawn of a cloud on the horizon. (pp. 18, 19)

It is this ability to respond without preconception to the relevant cloud of thought that we need to cultivate, and in Lyotard's assessment it is what was missing in his own career as a political militant (although we have noted the germ of it there at least, even in his earliest writings on the Algerian situation). We can learn from Cézanne's 'touch' (Lyotard deliberately plays on the various meanings of the English word with its connotations of, for example, lightness and sense of identification) how to respond to events, political no less than aesthetic: touch in art effectively equates to probity in philosophical thinking. As with the reference to 'lightness' of thought, 'touch' also brings svelteness to mind. Lyotard is not trying to claim that politics and art are cognate disciplines, merely that both 'are excepted, although in different ways, from the hegemony of the genre of discourse called cognitive'. There is a clear implication, however, that politics could only benefit from featuring something like Cézanne's lightness of touch in its practice; in each case what we have to listen for is 'the manifold contingency of data' (p. 21).

Twentieth-century experimental music, in its rejection of the idea of 'resolution' (Lyotard makes a suggestive link between tonal harmony and its drive to resolve discords, and modernity's ever-present desire for order), is singled out as another example of lightness of touch in action. A composer in this mould, Lyotard claims, proceeds 'without the goal of concluding or resolving his experiences, but rather with the intention of becoming unencumbered enough to meet events' (p. 25). Something of this latter quality of theoretical lightness is what is wanted in the world of politics too.

Lyotard's reading of his own militant past emphasizes the lack of touch, the incapacity to be sensitive to the contingency of the relevant data, and the theoretical encumbrances he brings to events. Events then are read through the prism of Marxist theory, with the young political militant becoming so intoxicated by dialectical materialism's explanatory power that he becomes totally convinced that only that theory can resolve the manifest contradictions of Algerian society. What Marxism causes Lyotard and his *Socialisme ou barbarie* colleagues to do is to assume before the event the form this resolution must take. In retrospect, what they should have been doing was noting what was unique about the Algerian situation rather than forcing it to conform to a pattern dictated by an abstract theory, a classic case of 'anticipating what the event will be in reference to a pre-text', when 'no predetermination exempts any thinking from the responsibility of responding to each case' (p. 27). To assume that responsibility is to exhibit the touch and probity that the singularity of events demands of the individual: it is to be a philosopher, or artist, rather than a mere intellectual. One might again object that Lyotard is being a bit harsh on himself here, and that his Algerian writings exhibit far more of that quality of probity than he is willing to admit thirty years later, but in the sense that Marxist principles still form the horizon to his thinking during his *Socialisme ou barbarie* phase, he is no doubt justified in seeing something less than full weight being given to the differend at the time.

'Gaps': What is at Stake

If there are similarities between the fields of politics and aesthetics there are also some crucial 'gaps', most notably that between 'doing' and 'feeling':

> The question is: is it possible to respond to the political and the esthetic in the same way – that is, in terms of an ability to be sensitive

to a 'It happens . . .' – when, on the one hand, what is at stake in
politics, is doing something, and, on the other, what is at stake in
esthetics and art is feeling something oneself or making other people
feel something? (p. 28)

The question is eventually answered in the negative, although
Lyotard does allow for the possibility of an aesthetic feeling in
politics. What separates the fields is the presence of an ethical
obligation within political activity (Kantian ethics being a key
point of reference for Lyotard here), with the obligation being
directed towards some communally desired end:

> every political deliberation and decision, either explicitly or implicitly,
> involves a reference to and, as much as possible, an answer to the issue
> of what 'we' ought to be or become in the present circumstances . . .
> Even if the obligation is pervaded by the contextual aspects of the
> situation, that is, even if the obligatory aspect is concealed beneath
> pressing necessities, it still remains that so-called reality has a chance
> of appearing as a hindrance only insomuch as it impedes purposive-
> ness and delays for a moment action being taken in response to the
> question of what we ought to be or become. (p. 35)

Art contains no such element of purposiveness (the idea of 'progress' hardly applies to it, for example), and aesthetic pleasure is
unconcerned with the fulfilment of needs. Aesthetic pleasure has,
in short, nothing to do with the Kantian 'faculty of desire', and we
can speak of aesthetic pleasure, but not of ethical pleasure: 'it is
useless and hopeless to anticipate any peace, any release or relaxa-
tion of the will, that is to say, any pleasure, in meeting the law and
obligation' (p. 36). In its lack of reference to any transcendental
object, the aesthetic response to the 'It happens' is closer to the
Lyotardean ideal.

The aesthetic response under scrutiny owes much to Kantian
theory (the synthesis of forms by the imagination, etc.), and
Lyotard proceeds to float the idea (given his cloud imagery, the
verb seems an apt one to employ) of a much freer kind of
aesthetics:

> a strange esthetics in which what supports the esthetic feeling is no
> longer the free synthesis of forms by the imagination . . . but the
> failure to synthesize. This lack of synthesis as concerns the faculty

corresponds to such names as '*das Unform*' or '*die Formlosigkeit*,' unform or formlessness, as concerns the object. It does not mean that the object must be monstrous, only that its form is no longer the point of esthetic feeling. (p. 41)

Aesthetics freed from the pre-text of form would be a significant step towards the ideal state of receptivity for the stream of events to which we are all subject; unstructured feeling (of lightness and touch) would replace formal preconception (one can see why Lyotard so often instances Sterne, with his foregrounding of sentiment, as a postmodern[3]). It would also be a significant step towards the dissolution of personal identity, the 'I', or 'strange hateful formation' as Lyotard so revealingly refers to it. One of the things that the peregrination in question is describing is a journey away from the sovereign 'I' (Lyotard slots into a long-running French tradition of suspicion regarding the individual subject in this respect[4]), which is seen to present a barrier to our ability to bear witness and acknowledge the pervasiveness of the differend in human affairs; the 'I' very much has a pre-text. Lyotard informs us that 'I have always had the dream of being able to describe a peregrination among forms freed from such a stable point, even if I don't know why' (p. 31), which certainly suggests a desire to escape from the confines of the rational self.

Lyotard also sounds quite close to Hume at this point. The latter's analysis of personal identity revealed the individual to be a mere bundle of perceptions with nothing tying them together into a coherent, enduring unit (there being no 'necessary connexion' between causes and effects). All that we experienced was the constant flow of impressions (Lyotard's event series), and personal identity as we had traditionally conceived of it (an entity with coherence over time) was in consequence something of a chimera. In common with Lyotard, Hume could see no way to extend our knowledge into the future: we had no justification for assuming that our theories could in any way predetermine the course of events, the linkage to future phrases remained very much open. The difference is that whereas Hume is clearly alarmed at this state of affairs, Lyotard eagerly embraces it. Hume feels himself obliged to backtrack from contingency (into 'custom'); Lyotard regards it as philosophy's duty to keep that contingency, the 'I don't know what', in full view at all times.

The artist's duty is a similar one to the philosopher's, to bear witness in her or his own area of activity: 'We must find new paths in order to approach new artistic clouds and new clouds of thought' (p. 43). Risk-taking, lightness, probity, touch and svelteness become the order of the day, and art can be a prime means of developing these qualities and keeping phrase linkages open: the case for politics remains more questionable. If Lyotard remains in some sense a monk, he also remains in some sense an artist.

The Inhuman

Time's effect on thought and theory is taken up in more detail in *The Inhuman: Reflections on Time*, a collection of commissioned lectures which Lyotard warns us not to treat as a political manifesto or philosophical treatise; rather,

> The suspicion they betray (in both senses of the word) is simple, although double: what if human beings, in humanism's sense, were in the process of, constrained into, becoming inhuman (that's the first part)? And (the second part), what if what is 'proper' to humankind were to be inhabited by the inhuman? (*In*, p. 2)

The first kind of inhumanity is the inhumanity of the system, or 'development', the goal of all science and technology in today's world; the second, 'the infinitely secret one of which the soul is hostage' (p. 2) as Lyotard poetically puts it, is the inhumanity of our social conditioning: the pressure to conform to prescribed modes of behaviour that is placed on all of us as we pass from childhood to adulthood. Lyotard worries about what is lost in each process, noting that the faster we develop the faster we forget, and that our conditioning into society has the effect of crushing 'what after the fact I find I have always tried, under diverse headings – work, figural, heterogeneity, dissensus, event, thing – to reserve: the unharmonizable' (p. 4). It is against these inhumanities, and their misappropriation of time, that *The Inhuman* is directed.

Given development's success in overcoming opposition (Lyotard suggests that it has rendered revolutionary politics all but redundant), the question he feels compelled to raise is 'what else remains as "politics" except resistance to the inhuman?' (p. 7).

Significantly, it is a resistance which will proceed from that aspect of us which resists 'harmonization' in the name of the community; hence Lyotard's continued championship of dissensus.

'Can Thought go on without a Body?'

One of the most extraordinary essays in the collection is 'Can Thought go on without a Body?', which poses the development versus dissensus conflict in a particularly striking way. It is cast in the form of two addresses by 'He' and 'She', the former a pro-development argument and the latter a series of objections from the 'resistance'. 'He' dismisses philosophical enquiry, with its refusal to reach definite conclusions, as ultimately pointless, and it is worth quoting at length the basis for this assessment:

> While we talk, the sun is getting older. It will explode in 4.5 billion years. It's just a little beyond the halfway point of its expected lifetime. It's like a man in his early forties with a life expectancy of eighty. With the sun's death your insoluble questions will be done with too. It's possible they'll stay unanswered right up to the end, flawlessly formulated, though now both grounds for raising such questions as well as the place to do this will no longer exist. You explain: it's impossible to think an end, pure and simple, of anything at all, since the end's a limit and to think it you have to be on both sides of that limit. So what's finished or finite has to be perpetuated in our thought if it's to be thought of as finished. Now this is true of limits belonging to thought. But after the sun's death there won't be a thought to know that its death took place. That, in my view, is the sole serious question to face humanity today. (pp. 8–9)

Clearly, neither a universalizing grand narrative nor the most probity-conscious philosopher or artist can do anything about an event such as this, since no matter what intellectual or political games we may play in the interim, 'In 4.5 billion years there will arrive the demise of your phenomenology and your utopian politics' (p. 9). Time, which was seen as a beneficent agent of change in *Per*, the means by which thought-clouds altered form and direction in unpredictable ways, thus generating the necessity for new enquiries to be instituted, is now transformed into the ultimate enemy of thought, and, indeed, all human activity. This is the limit against which development is posed, the only real challenge to its restless internal dynamic.

True to development's basic optimism 'He' is soon trying to find a solution to this apparently most intractable of differends. The task that faces mankind is a simple, if technologically daunting one, 'how to make thought without a body possible' (p. 13); and that is taken to be the real business of all contemporary scientific research. Striking though such a notion is, we can see how it simply rides roughshod over the concerns of little narratives. The idea that the preservation of thought should take precedence over discovering ways to alleviate the lot of individuals, whose experience of life can only extend over a few decades at best, is highly questionable. Most of mankind, for very good and very pressing reasons, cares more about the here-and-now than any event at such a remove in time as 4.5 billion years – the scale of development is certainly describable as inhuman. We might also note, contra-development (although given his comments about thought in *Per* I am not sure that Lyotard would necessarily share these sentiments), that some Eastern religions would want to argue the desirability of the *extinction* of thought – perhaps even to regard this, a return to emptiness, as thought's true destiny. But then, development is a quintessentially Western phenomenon, and therefore hooked on the notion of 'complexification' (contemporary techno-science is later to be defined in 'Matter and Time' as 'a complexification of matter' (p. 45)).

'She's' scepticism about the project is entirely understandable, although it is not dismissed completely out of hand (perhaps Lyotard really *is* exercised about the possible demise of thought?). What 'She' introduces into the debate is feeling (the body intruding again as it had in *LE*); for example, the element of 'suffering' that goes along with human thought. 'Thinking and suffering overlap', it is insisted, and there is always the sheer 'pain of thinking' to be taken into account (pp. 18, 19). Human thinking is not in fact a neatly programmable activity theoretically replicable by 'thinking-machines': 'In what we call thinking the mind isn't "directed" but suspended. You don't give it rules. You teach it to receive' (p. 19). Speaking on behalf of development, 'He' had described the body as merely 'the hardware of the complex technical device that is human thought' (p. 13), but the 'pain of thinking' belies such a reductive outlook (and keeps the body firmly on the philosophical agenda). And whatever thought may be it is not really analogous to programmable software, no matter how sophisticated that is. Harking back to the cloud imagery of *Per*, thought is described as 'irresolute', that is, as resistant to fixed meanings and positions (such as the binary oppositions of computer language). Thinking, as Lyotard had informed us in *Per*, is a matter of being attentive to the 'It happens', therefore 'the suffering of thinking is a suffering of time, of what happens' (p. 19). Development is to be rejected because it does not take that element of suffering into account, and suffering is essential to the project of resistance that Lyotard wants to promote. 'The unthought hurts because we're comfortable in what's already thought', hence the necessity for ensuring that the hurt continues to occur, because without it there will be no dissent to development's plans; 'suffering', as 'She' points out, 'doesn't have a good reputation in the technological megalopolis. Especially the suffering of thinking . . . There's a trend towards "play", if not performance'.

'She' also raises the gender issue, implying perhaps that development, that quintessentially imperialist notion with its desire for endless conquest and expansion, is to be identified with masculinity (a similar implication is to be noted in 'One of the Things at Stake in Women's Struggles'). Sexual difference is viewed as an 'incompleteness' deep inside us, 'of not just bodies, but minds too' (p. 20), that techno-science wishes to eradicate, or at least disguise, in the name of a system-enhancing neutrality (and what can be more neutral than a computer program?). There is even the possibility (if no more than that, it is hard to provide conclusive proof) that sexual difference may turn out to be an ontological difference, hence the source of differends. Techno-science invariably dislikes difference and differends, which it can only regard as a bar to efficiency, hence 'She's' insistence that sexual difference be retained in any attempt to extend thought beyond its time-limit: 'Your thinking machines will have to be nourished not just on radiation but on the irremediable differend of gender' (p. 22). Sexual difference becomes a critical element of resistance to development and its inhuman tendency towards neutralization.

Development equates to advanced capitalism, which Lyotard can no longer confront with the doctrines of Marxist theory. Post-Algeria and 1968 the Marxist route is closed to him, although unlike many ex-Marxists Lyotard has not succumbed to the embrace of capitalism and is still advocating resistance to it – if of a more diffuse type than in his Marxist days. Resistance now is an essentially local phenomenon, conducted at individual level through the foregrounding of psychological, sociological and sexual difference. Therein lies its weakness of course: the forces of techno-science are simply better organized than those of the scattered multitude of little narratives, no matter how resistant the latter may prove themselves to be individually. Nor is it all that easy to say what resistance by the foregrounding of difference and differends really means in terms of individual action: unplanned peregrinations of the Lyotard type, perhaps? One can applaud the sincerity but question the effectiveness of peregrinations in destabilizing the massed ranks of the techno-scientists and their political fellow-travellers.

'Time Today'

Lyotard is clearly haunted by development's supposed race against the end of the universe, and he returns to the theme in 'Time Today', an exploration of how contemporary techno-science deals with the factor of time. Once again, the concern is to show how development works to neutralize difference, and how inimical its process of complexification and rationalization ultimately is to the human spirit. The goal of techno-science is to enable 'its users to stock more information, to improve their competence and optimize their performances' (p. 62), and this is not, Lyotard suggests, a programme of emancipation as envisaged by modern metaphysical thought, but rather an inhuman drive towards the creation of 'the most complete monad' of which mankind is capable, in order to escape a dying solar system. As he remarks elsewhere, 'It is no longer possible to call development progress. It seems to proceed of its own accord . . . It does not answer to demands issuing from man's needs'.[5]

The more complete the monad the more complete its stock of information, and the more complete the stock of information the more neutralization of events has to take place (the 'I don't know what' disappears under this regime). Techno-science does not like the idea of the unknown or the unpredictable (the 'manifold contingency of data' offends its sense of order); it wants to control totally the way its process of complexification works in time, and,

> if one wants to control a process, the best way of doing so is to subordinate the present to what is (still) called the 'future', since in these conditions the 'future' will be completely predetermined and the present itself will cease opening onto an uncertain and contingent 'afterwards'. Better: what comes 'after' the 'now' will have to come 'before' it. In as much as a monad in thus saturating its memory is stocking the future, the present loses its privilege of being an ungraspable point from which, however, time should always distribute itself between the 'not yet' of the future and the 'no longer' of the past. (p. 65)

The elimination of unpredictability in the name of efficiency almost begins to look like the elimination of time itself, and thus even the possibility of difference. At the very least this is not the most promising of landscapes for humanity, and as Lyotard complains, 'among the events which the programme attempts to neutralize as much as it can one must, alas, also count the unforseeable effects engendered by the contingency and freedom proper to the human project' (p. 69).

The point of resistance is to keep that contingency and freedom intact, but the rather pessimistic tone of 'Time Today' makes one wonder just how viable that particular project remains. Lyotard writes from within a social context in which development seems to have infected almost all areas of human activity. Even thought itself has now been roped into the ultra-rational techno-scientific project of preparing for the end of the universe, whereas as far as Lyotard is concerned 'Being prepared to receive what thought is not prepared to think is what deserves the name of thinking' (p. 73). The commitment to the event and what it demands of us as individuals (probity, touch, svelteness, receptivity to the 'I don't know what') endures, although our scope to respond to the event seems to be progressively narrowing in the face of development's spreading, and to Lyotard essentially malign, influence. From that point of view *In* is not the most optimistic of works.

Development is a formidable enemy, to the extent that it has more or less usurped modern democracy in Lyotard's opinion. What is at stake in resistance to development's onwards march is nothing less than the preservation of the human race as we know it. 'When the point is to extend the capacities of the monad', Lyotard notes, 'it seems reasonable to abandon, or even actively to destroy, those parts of the human race which appear superfluous, useless for that goal' (p. 76). In a chilling aside that has considerable resonance in the current world political climate, he adds, 'For example, the populations of the Third World' (pp. 76–7), who are of course systematically excluded from almost all of the benefits of the techno-scientific revolution. Nor does one need to look as far as the Third World to find an example of this 'rationalization' in action: the deliberate marginalization of large segments of the population has been a distinctive feature of official economic policy in most Western societies throughout the 1980s and 1990s (long-term, possibly even permanent, unemployment being 'the price worth paying', as so many British Conservative politicians have assured us, to bring down inflation, create a more competitive market, 'smash socialism', etc.). Many commentators now see most developed economies as saddled with an apparently indefinitely disadvantaged underclass, whose disadvantage is a 'rational' requirement of the rest of society (effectively the basis of its own economic 'success'). Emotively enough, Lyotard sees such behaviour as being on a spectrum of inhumanity which also contains the Nazi extermination of the Jews (the other victims being 'the jews' spoken of in *Hj*).

What Lyotard is determined to guarantee, therefore, is 'the coming of the future in its unexpectedness' (p. 77), as well as our ability to respond and bear witness to the stream of events it brings in its train. Always we come back to the event and the 'now' (Lyotard's admiration for the work of Barnett Baruch Newman, the subject of one of *In*'s essays, is based on his belief that 'The purpose of a painting by Newman is not to show that duration is in excess of consciousness, but to be the occurrence, the moment which has arrived' (p. 79)); these have to be preserved in all their unpredictability from the neutralizing operations of development and techno-science; they are in fact inescapably part of what it means to be human. 'The question raised by the new technologies in connection with their relation to art is that of the here-and-now', Lyotard insists, going on to query,

> What does 'here' mean on the phone, on television, at the receiver of an electronic telescope? And the 'now'? Does not the 'tele-' element

necessarily destroy presence, the 'here-and-now' of the forms and
their 'carnal' reception? What is a place, a moment, not anchored in
the immediate 'passion' of what happens? Is a computer in any way
here and now? Can anything *happen* with it? Can anything happen *to*
it? (p. 118)

Ultimately, resistance is concerned to ensure that the world remains a place where events both happen and are experienced to
happen in a here-and-now which cannot be programmed be-
forehand: a world in which there continue to be 'I don't know
whats', where figures continue to disrupt discourses. Attentiveness
to time constitutes a critical element in the project of keeping both
forms of inhumanity at bay, and the 'reflections on time' are not
merely metaphysical but have a specifically political motivation.

Conclusion: Lyotard in perspective

Engagement with works like *In* indicates that Lyotard's thought is still evolving, although at the same time it also remains true to certain recurrent concerns of his career, such as the suspicion of authority, the desire to redress the unequal balance between individual and system, the mistrust of totalizing theory, and, indeed, the unremitting scepticism about the theoretical enterprise in general. These help us to put his career, for all its 'shifts and breaks', into some kind of perspective, and to speculate as to what his place ultimately might be in the history of philosophy.

I would suggest that what immediately strikes us about Lyotard as a philosopher is a rock-solid sense of honesty. One comes away from any prolonged exposure to his writings with an enormous respect for the honesty of his thought (as apparent in *In* as it is in the earliest of the Algerian writings), even if one does not always agree with where this trait can lead him. What can be said is that he is never one to back away from a crisis. The crisis in Lyotard's thought that comes to a head in the late 1960s/early 1970s (although as we have seen, presentiments of it are there far earlier) is one that many Western Marxists have had to undergo in the face of the theory's growing inability to cope with the radical changes – technological as well as socio-political – that have marked late twentieth-century life. Lyotard chose the hardest of routes out of

this morass: whereas some Marxists retreated back into the funda-
mentals of the theory as if they were matters of faith that could not
be affected greatly by the events of the real political world (where
the theory was running into increasing trouble), and others dis-
carded Marxism in favour of coming to some kind of an accom-
modation with the seemingly triumphant capitalist world order,
Lyotard opted to continue to resist capitalism with something like
the fervour of a Marxist believer – but without benefit of the
theory itself. Lyotard continues to suffer at the prospect of injustice but can no longer call on Marxism, a theory rooted in the
desire to correct injustice to humanity on the grand scale, for aid.
It is a particularly uncomfortable position to find oneself in as a
theorist.

To his credit, Lyotard adheres unflinchingly to his principles,
retaining his revolutionary outlook while refusing to modify his
implacable opposition to the Marxist establishment; neither lapsing into the embrace of a fundamentalist Marxism nor a techno-
science-driven capitalism. It can be a painful process to observe,
this enactment of Western thought in a period of accelerated
cultural crisis, and certainly the upheaval of the soul it has required of Lyotard is clear for all to see on the pages of *LE*, with its
'flesh and blood of words' only too palpably in evidence. I would
want to argue that Lyotard's refusal to take the easy way out of the
intractable situation in which he finds himself in the aftermath of
Algeria and 1968 (his very own legitimation crisis, in effect), has to
earn our respect, whether one is in agreement with his sentiments
or not.

Honesty alone is not enough to recommend a philosopher,
however, or to guarantee his future reputation, and Lyotard has
other, more weighty, claims to make on our attention. For a start,
his insistence on bringing the body back onto the philosophical
agenda (a concern he shares with Foucault) is to be congratulated.
Philosophy has for too long simply ignored this aspect of human
being. Then too, Lyotard has consistently been one of the most
inventive, as well as one of the most rigorous and tough-minded,
of anti-foundationalist thinkers, and the differend represents a
brave attempt to continue to engage with the issue of justice in a
world seemingly bereft of criteria for doing so. Lyotard deploys
the concept in an adroit enough way to keep at least some of the
charges of relativism at bay, and to give him his due, his sense of

the importance of Auschwitz as a catastrophic event in human history ought to deflect any charge of crude relativism against his thought: it has to be acknowledged that we are dealing with a morally very serious thinker who is never cavalier about the consequences of human action and is never an advocate of an amoral free-for-all in social existence. To bear witness to the differend between genres of discourse, as well as to the necessity of keeping phrase linkages open, is to respect the right to self-expression of the little narrative – which is always under the obligation not to encroach on the expression of other little narratives.

There is a strong ethical dimension to note to Lyotard's thought, therefore ('probity' is one of his ideals, after all), whose concern is to protect the status of the little narrative against interference by outside forces: the anti-authoritarianism indeed runs deep. Whether the tactics that Lyotard offers to the little narrative (svelteness, probity, bearing witness, the 'here-and-now kind' of political action, etc.) are in themselves enough to resist the power of grand narrative, or its more sinister replacement in late twentieth-century society, a techno-scientific capitalism bent on massive expansion, is another matter; certainly *In* is not the most optimistic of works on that score, with its bleak picture of a world order inexorably geared towards the preservation of thought at the expense of all other considerations, with no other opposition than a small band of dissidents.

Nevertheless, one can still applaud a concern with the little narrative that stretches back to Lyotard's politically militant days, where his sympathy with the individual Algerian being used as a pawn by self-interested larger forces is both unmistakable and highly perceptive in terms of the revolution's ultimate fate (and as I write in the mid-1990s, Algeria is in the grip of something like a civil war, which suggests just how widespread the revolution's failings have been). Lyotard's anti-foundationalism is motivated, not by some abstract metaphysics (a criticism often made of Derrida, for example), but by a sincere desire for a better deal for the individual in his or her relationship to the socio-political system, for justice in something other than the narrow legal sense traditionally sanctioned by that system.

For the time being at least Lyotard is still very closely identified in the public mind with postmodernism, and as long as that remains a talking point his name will be prominent in the domain of cultural critique. Lyotard has made some striking contributions to postmodern thought. His conception of postmodernism as a cyclical phenomenon has opened up the past to analysis, thus complementing Charles Jencks's appropriation of the past for the postmodern ethos in the theory of double coding. Whereas modernity usually involved a decisive break with past cultural practices, an attitude that is still with us in contemporary techno-science and its urge to keep developing beyond current frontiers of knowledge, postmodernism, through the efforts of thinkers like Lyotard and Jencks, has kept the lines of dialogue open with the past, thus acting as a brake on the wilder excesses of modernity and its offspring, capitalism. We can say of Lyotardean postmodernism in particular that it is acutely historically conscious, if in a very different way to the grand narratives (Marxism, for example) it has sought actively to undermine. Lyotard suggests, for example, that postmodernism in the arts, philosophy and politics is like a form of psychoanalytic therapy, whereby hidden meanings in Western cultural history are brought to the surface, thus breaking a cycle of repression:

> the 'post-' of 'postmodern' does not signify a movement of *comeback*, *flashback* or *feedback*, that is, not a movement of repetition but a procedure in 'ana-': a procedure of analysis, anamnesis, anagogy and anamorphosis which elaborates an 'initial forgetting'.[1]

What that 'ana' recovers is an awareness of figure, libidinal economy, differend, etc., all those ultimately uncontainable forces that Western discourse tries so hard to hide from itself, at so great cost to so many little narratives.

From a more critical standpoint, Lyotard's identification of modernisms and postmodernisms in the past can too easily turn into a facile game – Sterne is a postmodernist, but Descartes, on the other hand, is a modernist, and so on – which runs the risk of losing sight of our differences with the past (especially the remote past of, say, classical Greece), and, perhaps, trivializing its concerns by viewing it through recent theoretical perspectives.

Lyotard's recasting of ideologies as grand narratives governed by their own particular brand of narrative pragmatics has exercised a profound effect on recent political and theoretical discourse. It holds out the possibility of rapid, and radical, change once those pragmatics are met with incredulity rather than, as was so often the case in modernism, a sense of individual powerlessness in the face of the system's defence mechanisms. Incredulity becomes a powerful weapon to wield against grand narrative monopoly, a weapon to which the latter has no very effective response. One can point to cases of incredulity towards grand narratives having the desired effect of the narrative's collapse in recent history: the relatively sudden disappearance of Communist hegemony in Russia and Eastern Europe being one such outstanding example. Against Lyotard, one can point out that grand narratives can have considerable resilience to incredulity, and that they will not always necessarily implode under the weight of their own contradictions. The rise of religious fundamentalism in recent decades is a worrying phenomenon in this respect to anyone dedicated to the battle against intolerance of individual and cultural difference (and grand narratives are not particularly noted for their qualities of toleration), as well as a sign of grand narrative's continuing hold over the popular imagination; it has to be conceded that grand narrative is meeting some deep psychological need that postmodernism is perhaps not being particularly sensitive to, or simply failing to acknowledge as a significant cultural factor. Neither does Lyotard accord enough weight to the perceived advantages of grand narratives: their sense of involving the individual in a cause larger than his or her own, thus empowering him or her, and of offering solidarity with his or her fellow human beings. Not everyone has the strength of character for the somewhat rugged, and certainly highly principled, individualism demanded by Lyotard's philosophical politics ('Are you prejudging the *Is it happening?*'), with its endless obligation to bear witness, exhibit probity and remain in a state of svelte wakefulness, and not everyone can face up to the challenge of an existence without rules or criteria of judgement; nor is the unknown, the 'I don't know what', as great an attraction to the public at large as it manifestly is to Lyotard.

Lyotard will almost certainly go down as an important figure in the history of Marxism – if of a negative type. Few ex-Marxists have unleashed such a vicious attack on the theory as Lyotard did in *LE* (surely nowhere are the 'extreme consequences' of the *Socialisme ou barbarie* ethos more completely realized, even if Lyotard had long since broken with the movement): an attack all the more memorable given the author's continued, and unmistakably sincere anti-capitalism. *LE* has to be considered one of the most effective critiques (crudely put though it is) of the notion of false consciousness, and Lyotard succeeds in posing some very awkward questions for the left, which has no other very convincing way of explaining the rightward turn in Western politics in the last couple of decades, in this respect. Postmodernism, particularly the 'red in tooth and claw' version of it to be found in *LE*, ought to make the left rethink large areas of its policy – as well as its attitude towards the working class. Lyotard-the-postmodernist can still muster a certain admiration for Marx, who at least initially bore witness to the differend, but not for many Marxists, who in Lyotard's reading become hopelessly entangled in a project of universalization that is doomed at source.

Above all else Lyotard remains a deeply political thinker – arguably the most political of the poststructuralists – whose concern to keep philosophy relevant to everyday affairs is consistently evident throughout his considerable body of writings (in that sense the 'many and various Lyotards' are one), and that is a rare enough quality to be worthy of acclaim. When it comes to 'the question of power', Lyotard has few peers amongst contemporary analysts.

Notes

Preface

1. Geoffrey Bennington, *Lyotard: Writing the Event*, Manchester: Manchester University Press, 1988, p.1.
2. Jean-François Lyotard, *Libidinal Economy*, translated by Iain Hamilton Grant, London: Athlone Press, 1993, p. 259. All further page references will be given in parentheses within the text.
3. Bill Readings, *Introducing Lyotard: Art and Politics*, London and New York: Routledge, 1991.

Historical and cultural context

1. Jean-François Lyotard, *Phenomenology*, translated by Brian Beakley, Albany, NY: State University of New York Press, 1991, p. 123. All further page references will be given in parentheses within the text.
2. See Jacques Derrida, *Spectres of Marx: The State of the Debt, the Work of Mourning, and the New International*, translated by Peggy Kamuf, New York and London: Routledge, 1994.
3. Jean-François Lyotard, 'A Svelte Appendix to the Postmodern Question', in Jean-François Lyotard, *Political Writings*, translated by Bill Readings and Kevin Paul Geiman, London: UCL Press, 1993, p. 28 (from Jean-François Lyotard, *Tombeau de l'intellectuel et autres papiers*, Paris: Galilee, 1984). All further page references will be given in parentheses within the text.

144

4. For Gayle L. Ormiston, for example, the text is marked by 'differends that provoke and orient its reflections', and she speculates also whether Lyotard's 'phenomenological episode is the condition of the postmodern conceived too soon?' (Foreword, *Ph*, pp. 5, 16).
5. Louis Althusser and Étienne Balibar, *Reading Capital*, translated by Ben Brewster, London: NLB, 1970, and *For Marx*, translated by Ben Brewster, London: NLB, 1977. For a history of the structural Marxist movement see Ted Benton, *The Rise and Fall of Structural Marxism*, London and Basingstoke: Macmillan, 1984.
6. Peter Dews, *Logics of Disintegration: Post-structuralist Thought and the Claims of Critical Theory*, London and New York: Verso, 1987, p. 143.

Chapter 1

1. *Lyotard: Writing the Event*, Manchester: Manchester University Press, 1988, p. 9.
2. Jean-François Lyotard, *Political Writings*, translated by Bill Readings and Kevin Paul Geiman, London: UCL Press, 1993, p. 326. All further page references will be given in parentheses within the text.
3. The line argued by, for example, Georg Lukács in *History and Class Consciousness*, translated by Rodney Livingstone, London: Merlin Press, 1971.
4. From Jean-François Lyotard, *Dérive à partir de Marx et Freud*, Paris: Union Générale d'Éditions, 1973.
5. From *ibid.*
6. From *ibid.*
7. For more on situationism see Sadie Plant, *The Most Radical Gesture*, London: Routledge, 1992.
8. Foreword, *PW*, p. xxiii.
9. *PW*, p. 135.
10. Jean-François Lyotard, *Heidegger and 'the jews'*, translated by Andreas Michel and Mark Roberts, Minneapolis: University of Minnesota Press, 1990, p. 51. All further page references will be given in parentheses within the text.

Chapter 2

1. Jean-François Lyotard, *Peregrinations: Law, Form, Event*, New York: Columbia University Press, p. 13. All further page references will be given in parentheses within the text.
2. Iain Hamilton Grant, Introduction to *Libidinal Economy*, p. xvii.
3. For an argument playing down Lyotard's anti-Marxism, see Barry Smart, *Modern Conditions: Postmodern Controversies*, London and New York: Routledge, 1992. Smart's line is that, in Lyotard's work, 'Marxism is not so much renounced as qualified, circumscribed, and limited in its relevance to

capitalism' (pp. 204–5), although I must say I do not see how such a sentiment could survive exposure to *LE*'s quite vitriolic attack on the Marxist
cause.
4. David Carroll, *Paraesthetics: Foucault, Lyotard, Derrida*, London and New
York: Methuen, 1987, p. 44.
5. Jean-François Lyotard, 'The Dream-Work Does Not Think', in Andrew
Benjamin, ed., *The Lyotard Reader*, Oxford and Cambridge, MA: Blackwell,
1989, p. 19 (from Jean-François Lyotard, *Discours, figure*, Paris: Klinckseick,
1971). All further page references will be given in parentheses within the
text.
6. *Logics of Disintegration: Post-structuralist Thought and the Claims of Critical
Theory*, London and New York: Verso, 1987, p. 138.
7. *Per*, pp. 45–75, translated by Cecile Lindsay.

Chapter 3

1. Originally published in *Critique*, 419 (1982).
2. Jean-François Lyotard, *The Postmodern Condition: A Report on Knowledge*,
translated by Geoffrey Bennington and Brian Massumi, Manchester: Manchester University Press, 1984, pp. xxiii–xxiv. All further page references
will be given in parentheses within the text.
3. Lyotard returns to the subject of the Cashinahua in Jean-François Lyotard
and Jean-Loup Thébaud, *Just Gaming*, translated by Wlad Godzich (with
Afterword by Samuel Weber, translated by Brian Massumi), Manchester:
Manchester University Press, 1985, pp. 32–5, and also in Jean-François
Lyotard, *The Differend: Phrases in Dispute*, translated by Georges Van Den
Abbeele, Manchester: Manchester University Press, 1988, pp. 152–7. All
further page references to both works will be given in parentheses within the
text. For a critical reading of Lyotard's use of the Cashinahua from a postcolonial perspective, see Homi K. Bhabha, *The Location of Culture*, London
and New York: Routledge, 1994, where it is seen as 'part of a strategy of
containment where the Other text is forever the exegetical horizon of difference, never the active agent of articulation' (p. 31).
4. See, for example, Books 2, 3 and 10 of *The Republic*, where poets are
threatened with expulsion from Plato's ideal commonwealth if they dare to
mock state authority.
5. For more on chaos theory, see James Gleick, *Chaos: Making a New Science*,
London: Sphere, 1988.
6. See *ibid.*, pp. 94–6.
7. I discuss the anti-foundational trend in recent French thought in Stuart Sim,
Beyond Aesthetics: Confrontations with Poststructuralism and Postmodernism,
Hemel Hempstead: Harvester Wheatsheaf, 1992.
8. For an argument challenging the notion of *PC*'s political 'attractiveness', see
John Keane, 'The Modern Democratic Revolution: Reflections on Lyotard's
The Postmodern Condition', in Andrew Benjamin, ed., *Judging Lyotard*, Lon-
don and New York: Routledge, 1992, pp. 81–98. For Keane, *PC* is 'marked

by a profound uncertainty and lack of clarity about its socio-political affilia-
tions' (p. 90).

9. 'Freud, Duchamp, Bohr, Gertrude Stein, but before them Rabelais and
Sterne, are postmoderns in that they stress paradoxes, which always attest the
incommensurability of which I am speaking' ('A Svelte Appendix', *PW*,
p. 28).

10. Margaret A. Rose provides a useful guide to the various interpretations of
'postmodernism' in 'Post-modern pastiche', *British Journal of Aesthetics*, 31
(1991), pp. 26–35.

11. 'Double coding' is defined as 'the combination of modern techniques with
something else (usually traditional building) in order for architecture to
communicate with the public and a concerned minority, usually other archi-
tects' (Charles Jencks, *What is Post-Modernism?*, London/New York: Acad-
emy Editions/St. Martin's Press, 1986, p. 14).

12. See, for example, *America*, translated by Chris Turner, London and New
York: Verso, 1988, and *Cool Memories*, translated by Chris Turner, London
and New York: Verso, 1990.

Chapter 4

1. See, for example, Christopher Norris's analysis of the rhetorical strategies of
a selection of modern philosophers in *The Deconstructive Turn: Essays in the
Rhetoric of Philosophy*, London and New York: Methuen, 1983.

2. Similar complaints have been made about Jacques Derrida. Thus David
Wood's comment that, for many, Derrida is engaged in 'the production of an
invulnerable discourse' that renders it 'completely immune to criticism'
(David Wood, 'Following Derrida', in John Sallis, ed., *Deconstruction and
Philosophy: The Texts of Jacques Derrida*, Chicago and London: Chicago
University Press, 1987, pp. 143–60 (p. 158)).

3. See David Hume, *A Treatise of Human Nature*, ed. D. G. C. Macnabb,
Glasgow: Fontana/Collins, 1962, and *An Enquiry Concerning Human Under-
standing*, ed. L. A. Selby-Bigge, rev. P. H. Nidditch, Oxford: Clarendon
Press, 1975.

4. 'Either a narrative is merely a rambling collection of events, in which case
nothing can be said about it other than by referring back to the storyteller's
(the author's) art, talent or genius – all mythical forms of chance – or else it
shares with other narratives a common structure which is open to analysis, no
matter how much patience its formulation requires' (Roland Barthes, *Image-
Music-Text*, translated by Stephen Heath, Glasgow: Fontana/Collins, 1977,
p. 80).

5. '. . . Lyotard, who at times is mistakenly represented as an *advocate* rather
than an *analyst* of the postmodern condition' (Barry Smart, *Modern Conditions: Postmodern Controversies*, London and New York: Routledge, 1992,
p. 204). Smart's reading does admittedly ring true on occasion. In *PC* we can
say that Lyotard is analysing, and clearly bemoaning rather than advocating,
the power of the multinationals in determining the direction of scientific

research. Eagleton for one misses this distinction, arguing that as far as Lyotard is concerned 'he who has the fattest research grant is most likely to be right' (Terry Eagleton, *The Ideology of the Aesthetic*, Oxford and Cambridge, MA: Blackwell, 1990, p. 396).

6. For a reading emphasizing Lyotard's debt to sophism, see Arthur Kroker, *The Possessed Individual: Technology and Postmodernism*, Basingstoke: Macmillan, 1992, where it is argued that Lyotard's thought 'is a systematic working-out of the sophist's imagination' (p. 144).

7. See Friedrich Nietzsche, *The Will to Power*, translated by Walter Kaufmann and R. J. Hollingdale, London: Weidenfeld and Nicolson, 1968.

Chapter 5

1. *Lyotard: Writing the Event*, Manchester: Manchester University Press, 1988, p. 2.

2. Geoffrey Bennington prefers 'sentence' in *Writing the Event*, for example.

3. 'In one sense choice is possible, but what is not possible is not to choose. I can always choose, but I must know that if I do not choose, that is still a choice' (Jean-Paul Sartre, *Existentialism and Humanism*, translated by Philip Mairet, London: Methuen, 1973, p. 48).

4. *Cogito ergo sum* being taken to be a disprovable proposition, while the *epoché*, the reduction of the world-out-there to the individual's stream of sense experiences, provides a presuppositionless (therefore in Husserl's view, unassailable) starting-point for philosophical discourse

5. See Geoffrey Bennington, *Writing the Event*, for an extended treatment of Lyotard's preoccupation with the event.

6. See Barry Smart, *Modern Conditions: Postmodern Controversies*, London and New York: Routledge, 1992, pp. 204–5, for example.

7. For an interesting application of the differend to territorial politics, see Bill Readings, 'Pagans, Perverts or Primitives? Experimental Justice in the Empire of Capital', in Andrew Benjamin, ed., *Judging Lyotard*, London and New York: Routledge, 1992, pp. 168–91, where the case of the Australian Aborigines is considered.

8. This debate still rages in the 1990s. See, for example, Deborah Lipstadt, *Denying the Holocaust: The Growing Assault on Truth and Memory*, Harmondsworth: Penguin, 1994, and Lawrence D. Kritzman, ed., *Auschwitz and After: Race, Culture, and 'The Jewish Question' in France*, London and New York: Routledge, 1994.

9. Quoted in *Diff*, p. 3.

10. See Bishop George Berkeley, *The Principles of Human Knowledge* and *Three Dialogues between Hylas and Philonous* in A. A. Luce and T. E. Jessop, eds, *The Works of George Berkeley*, vols I–IX (vol. II), London: Thomas Nelson, 1949.

11. See, for example, Michel Foucault, *Madness and Civilization*, translated by Richard Howard, London: Tavistock, 1967, and *Discipline and Punish*, translated by Alan Sheridan, Harmondsworth: Penguin, 1977.

12. Derrida consistently argues against the idea of there being fixed origins or foundations for discourse. Everywhere we look in a discourse, he claims, we find merely traces of previous traces. The *mis en abyme*, with its infinite regress of smaller versions of an image contained with the larger image, provides a more realistic guide to the structure of things.

13. For the Marxist commentator Alex Callinicos, for example, Lyotardean postmodernism constitutes 'a rationale for lying back and enjoying late capitalism' (Alex Callinicos, 'Reactionary Postmodernism?', in Roy Boyne and Ali Rattansi, eds, *Postmodernism and Society*, New York: St. Martin's Press, 1990, p. 114).

Chapter 6

1. 'A Svelte Appendix', in *PW*, pp. 25–9. All further page references will be given in parentheses within the text.

2. Jean-François Lyotard, *The Inhuman: Reflections on Time*, translated by Geoffrey Bennington and Rachel Bowlby, Cambridge/Oxford: Polity Press/ Blackwell, 1991, p. 105. All further page references will be given in parentheses within the text.

3. 'Lessons in Paganism', translated by David Macey, in *LR*, pp. 122–54.

4. 'Futility in Revolution', in Jean-François Lyotard, *Toward the Postmodern*, eds Robert Harvey and Mark S. Roberts, Atlantic Highlands, NJ and London: Humanities Press, 1993, p. 111 (from Jean-François Lyotard, *Rudiments païens: genre dissertatif*, Paris: Union Générale d'Éditions, 1977).

5. 'One of the Things at Stake in Women's Struggles', translated by Deborah J. Clarke, Winifred Woodhull and John Mowitt, in *LR*, pp. 111–21 (p. 120) (from *Rudiments païens*).

Chapter 7

1. Jean-François Lyotard, *Lessons on the Analytic of the Sublime*, translated by Elizabeth Rottenberg, Stanford, CA: Stanford University Press, 1994, p. ix. All further page references will be given in parentheses within the text.

2. '. . . this pagan resides in an infiltration – at the surface of the social body – of . . . areas left open to the instincts' ('Futility in Revolution', *TP*, p. 99).

Chapter 8

1. For a critique of this exhibition see Paul Crowther, '*Les Immatériaux* and the Postmodern Sublime', in Andrew Benjamin, ed., *Judging Lyotard*, London and New York: Routledge, 1992, pp. 192–205.

2. *Paraesthetics: Foucault, Lyotard, Derrida*, London: Methuen, 1987, p. 30.

3. Jean-François Lyotard, *Duchamp's Trans/Formers*, translated by I. McLeod, Venice, CA: The Lapis Press, 1990, p. 87. All further page references will be given in parentheses within the text.
4. *LR*, pp. 220–39, translated by David Macey (from *Catalogue ADAMI*, Paris: Éditions du Centre Georges Pompidou, 1985).
5. *LR*, pp. 169–80, translated by Paisley N. Livingstone (from *Des dispositifs pulsionnels*, Paris: Union Générale d'Éditions, 1973).

Chapter 9

1. An illustrative example of the status accorded French intellectuals can be found in the UNESCO-sponsored 1950 film *La Vie commence demain* (*Life Begins Tomorrow*), a blend of fact and fiction in which an Everyman figure (played by the actor Jean-Pierre Aumont) goes the rounds of a selection of high-profile intellectuals, including Sartre, seeking their advice on how best to live in a difficult postwar world. Intellectuals are portrayed in the film as sources of wisdom for the common good.
2. *PW*, pp. 3–29.
3. *Ibid.*, pp. 90–5.
4. 'One of the Things at Stake in Women's Struggles', *LR*, p. 118.

Chapter 10

1. If anything Rorty is even more adamant about the value of literature than Lyotard is: 'This process of coming to see other human beings as "one of us" rather than as "them" is a matter of detailed description of what unfamiliar people are like and of redescription of what we ourselves are like. This is a task not for theory but for genres such as ethnography, the journalist's report, the comic book, the docudrama, and, especially, the novel' (Richard Rorty, *Contingency, Irony, Solidarity*, Cambridge: Cambridge University Press, 1989, p. xvi).
2. Thus Terry Eagleton's remark, apropos Lyotard's theory of narrative, that, 'It is also hard to see how this move would not, for example, authorize the narratives of Nazism, provided they are grippingly enough recounted' (*Ideology of the Aesthetic*, Oxford and Cambridge, MA: Blackwell, 1990, p. 396).
3. Sentiment for Sterne is the only way left of coping with a chaotic world full of unpredictable events (the product of either fate or chance) that rationality can neither foresee nor satisfactorily explain (see *Tristram Shandy* or *A Sentimental Journey*).
4. Lévi-Strauss, Barthes, Foucault, Deleuze and Guattari, and Derrida have all in their own way celebrated the death of the subject. As Foucault puts it, 'As the archaeology of our thought easily shows, man is an invention of recent date. And perhaps one nearing its end' (Michel Foucault, *The Order of Things: An Archaeology of the Human Sciences*, translated by Alan Sheridan-Smith, New York: Random House, 1970, p. 387).

5. Jean-François Lyotard, *The Postmodern Explained to Children: Correspondence 1982–1985*, translated by Don Barry et al., edited by Julian Pefanis and Morgan Thomas, London: Turnaround, 1992, pp. 91–2.

Conclusion

1. *The Postmodern Explained to Children: Correspondence 1982–1985*, translated by Don Barry et al., edited by Julian Pefanis and Morgan Thomas, London: Turnaround, 1992, p. 93.

Select bibliography

Main published works of Jean-François Lyotard

La Phénoménologie, Paris: Presses Universitaires de France, 1954.
Discours, figure, Paris: Klinckseick, 1971.
Dérive à partir de Marx et Freud, Paris: Union Générale d'Éditions, 1973.
Des dispositifs pulsionnels, Paris: Union Générale d'Éditions, 1973.
Economie libidinale, Paris: Les Éditions de Minuit, 1974.
Instructions païennes, Paris: Galilée, 1977.
Récits tremblants, Paris: Galilée, 1977.
Rudiments païens: genre dissertatif, Paris: Union Générale d'Éditions, 1977.
Les Transformateurs Duchamp, Paris: Galilée, 1977.
Le Mur du pacifique, Paris: Galilée, 1979.
Au Juste (with Jean-Loup Thébaud), Paris: Christian Bourgeois, 1979.
La Condition postmoderne, Paris: Minuit, 1979.
Sur la constitution du temps par la couleur dans les oeuvres récentes d'Albert Aymé, Paris: Éditions Traversière, 1980.
Le Différend, Paris: Minuit, 1983.
L'Assassinat de l'expérience par la peinture: Monory, Paris: Castor Astral, 1984.
Driftworks, translated by Roger McKeon, Susan Hanson, Ann Knab, Richard Lockwood and Joseph Maier. New York: Columbia University Press, 1984.
Tombeau de l'intellectuel et autres papiers, Paris: Galilée, 1984.
Le Postmoderne expliqué aux enfants: Correspondance 1982–1985, Paris: Galilée, 1986.
L'Enthousiasme: la critique kantienne de l'histoire, Paris: Galilée, 1986.

Que Peindre? Adami Arakawa Buren, Paris: Éditions de la Différence, 1987.
Heidegger et 'les juifs', Paris: Galilée, 1988.
Peregrinations: Law, Event, Form, New York: Columbia University Press, 1988.
L'inhumain: Causeries sur le temps, Paris: Galilée, 1988.
La Guerre des Algériens: Écrits 1956–63, Paris: Galilée, 1988.
Leçons sur l'analytique du sublime, Paris: Galilée, 1991.
Lectures d'enfance, Paris: Galilée, 1991.
Moralités postmodernes, Paris: Galilée, 1993.

English translations of Jean-François Lyotard

The Differend: Phrases in Dispute, translated by George Van Den Abbeele, Manchester: Manchester University Press, 1988.
Duchamp's Trans/Formers, translated by I. McLeod, Venice, CA: The Lapis Press, 1990.
Heidegger and 'the jews', translated by Andreas Michel and Mark Roberts, Minneapolis: University of Minnesota Press, 1990.
The Inhuman: Reflections on Time, translated by Geoffrey Bennington and Rachel Bowlby, Oxford: Blackwell, 1991.
Just Gaming, translated by Wlad Godzich, Manchester: Manchester University Press, 1985.
Lessons on the Analytic of the Sublime, translated by Elizabeth Rottenberg, Stanford, CA: Stanford University Press, 1994.
Libidinal Economy, translated by Iain Hamilton Grant, London: Athlone Press, 1993.
The Lyotard Reader, edited by Andrew Benjamin, Oxford and Cambridge, MA: Blackwell, 1989.
Phenomenology, translated by Brian Beakley, Albany, NY: State University of New York Press, 1991.
Political Writings, translated by Bill Readings and Kevin Paul Geiman, London: UCL Press, 1993.
The Postmodern Condition: A Report on Knowledge, translated by Geoffrey Bennington and Brian Massumi, Manchester: Manchester University Press, 1984.
The Postmodern Explained to Children: Correspondence 1982–1985, translated by Don Barry, Bernadette Maher, Julian Pefanis, Virginia Spate and Morgan Thomas, edited by Julian Pefanis and Morgan Thomas, London: Turnaround, 1992.
Toward the Postmodern, edited by Robert Harvey and Mark S. Roberts, Atlantic Highlands, NJ and London: Humanities Press International, 1993.

Studies of Jean-François Lyotard

Agyros, Alex, 'Narrative and Chaos', *New Literary History*, 23 (1992), pp. 659–73.

Benjamin, Andrew, ed., *Judging Lyotard*, London and New York: Routledge, 1992.

Bennington, Geoffrey, *Lyotard: Writing the Event*, Manchester: Manchester University Press, 1988.

Callinicos, Alex, *Against Postmodernism: A Marxist Perspective*, Cambridge: Polity Press, 1989.

Carroll, David, *Paraesthetics: Foucault, Lyotard, Derrida*, London: Methuen, 1987.

Descombes, Vincent, *Modern French Philosophy*, translated by L. Scott-Fox and J. M. Harding, Cambridge and New York: Cambridge University Press, 1980.

Dews, Peter, *Logics of Disintegration: Post-structuralist Thought and the Claims of Critical Theory*, London and New York: Verso, 1987.

Jameson, Fredric, *Postmodernism, or, the Cultural Logic of Late Capitalism*, London: Verso, 1991.

Kreiswirth, Martin, 'Trusting the Tale: The Narrativist Turn in the Human Sciences', *New Literary History*, 23 (1992), pp. 629–57.

Kroker, Arthur, *The Possessed Individual: Technology and Postmodernity*, Basingstoke: Macmillan, 1992.

Nicholls, Peter, 'Divergences: Modernism, Postmodernism, Jameson and Lyotard', *Critical Quarterly*, 33 (1991), pp. 1–18.

Pefanis, Julian, *Heterology and the Postmodern: Bataille, Baudrillard, and Lyotard*, Durham and London: Duke University Press, 1991.

Poster, Mark, 'Postmodernity and the Politics of Multiculturalism: The Lyotard–Habermas Debate over Social Theory', *Modern Fiction Studies*, 38 (1992), pp. 567–80.

Raffel, Stanley, *Habermas, Lyotard and the Concept of Justice*, Basingstoke: Macmillan, 1992.

Readings, Bill, *Introducing Lyotard: Art and Politics*, London and New York: Routledge, 1991.

Rorty, Richard, 'Habermas and Lyotard on Postmodernity', in Ingeborg Hoesterey, ed., *Zeitgeist in Babel: The Postmodernist Controversy*, Bloomington and Indianapolis: Indiana University Press, 1991, pp. 84–97.

Sarup, Madan, *An Introductory Guide to Post-structuralism and Postmodernism*, Hemel Hempstead: Harvester Wheatsheaf, 1990; revised edition, 1993.

Segal, Alex, 'Language Games and Justice', *Textual Practice*, 6 (1992), pp. 210–24.

Sim, Stuart, *Beyond Aesthetics: Confrontations with Poststructuralism and Postmodernism*, Hemel Hempstead: Harvester Wheatsheaf, 1992.

Sim, Stuart, 'Svelte Discourse and the Philosophy of Caution', *Radical Philosophy*, 49 (1988), pp. 31–6.

Smart, Barry, *Modern Conditions, Postmodern Controversies*, London and New York: Routledge, 1992.

Index

155